AAL-7577

Meaning in everyday thought and language is constructed at lightning speed. We are not conscious of the staggering complexity of the cognitive operations that drive our simplest behavior. This book examines a central component of meaning construction; the mappings that link mental spaces. A deep result of the research is the fact that the same principles operate at the highest levels of scientific, artistic, and literary thought as do the lower levels of elementary understanding and sentence meaning. Some key cognitive operations are analogical mappings, conceptual integration and blending, discourse management, induction, and recursion.

The analyses are based on a rich array of attested data in ordinary language, humor, action and design, science, and narratives. Phenomena that receive attention include counterfactuals; time, tense, and mood; opacity; metaphor; fictive motion; grammatical constructions; and quantification over cognitive domains.

D1474588

Mappings in Thought
and Language

Mappings in Thought and Language

GILLES FAUCONNIER
University of California, San Diego

CAMBRIDGE
UNIVERSITY PRESS

PUBLISHED BY THE PRESS SYNDICATE OF THE UNIVERSITY OF CAMBRIDGE
The Pitt Building, Trumpington Street, Cambridge CB2 1RP, United Kingdom

CAMBRIDGE UNIVERSITY PRESS
The Edinburgh Building, Cambridge CB2 2RU, United Kingdom
40 West 20th Street, New York, NY 10011–4211, USA
10 Stamford Road, Oakleigh, Melbourne 3166, Australia

First published 1997

Printed in the United States of America

Typeset in Times Roman and Folio Medium

Library of Congress Cataloging-in-Publication Data
Fauconnier, Gilles.
Mappings in thought and language / Gilles Fauconnier.
p.   cm.
Includes bibliographical references (p.   ).
ISBN 0-521-46062-X (hardcover) – ISBN 0-521-59953-9 (pbk)
1. Meaning (Psychology).   2. Schemas (Psychology).   3. Cognitive
maps (Psychology).   4. Psycholinguistics.   I. Title.
BF463.M4F38   1997
153.4–dc20   96-23820
                                                      CIP

*A catalogue record for this book is available from
the British Library.*

ISBN 0 521 46062 X hardback
ISBN 0 521 59953 9 paperback

for Tina

The aspects of things that are most important for us are hidden because of their simplicity and familiarity.

—Wittgenstein, *Philosophical Investigations*

Contents

Acknowledgments

I am grateful and indebted to the many people who have helped and encouraged me in multiple ways, direct or indirect, to carry out the research reported on in this book.

- To Tina Huynh Fauconnier, to whom the book is dedicated, for her support and her deep insights into human thought and human nature.
- To my friends and coworkers who have significantly advanced our understanding of mental spaces and related phenomena: Aintzane Doiz-Bienzobas, Seana Coulson, Michelle Cutrer, John Dinsmore, Pierre Encrevé, Jeff Lansing, Scott Liddell, Nili Mandelblit, Errapel Mejías-Bikandi, Jo Rubba, Eve Sweetser, Shigeru Sakahara, Yuki Takubo, and Karen Van Hoek.
- To pioneers and fellow-travelers in cognitive semantics, George Lakoff, Ron Langacker, Claudia Brugman, and Len Talmy, whose influence is apparent throughout this book.
- To Mark Turner, my accomplice in giving scientific life to exotic manifestations of language.
- To Doug Hofstadter, for his inspiring work on analogy and other forms of thought.
- To Aaron Cicourel, for his generous guidance and key ideas.
- To Pierre Bourdieu, Benoît de Cornulier, Oswald Ducrot, and the late Erving Goffman, for the powerful intellectual frameworks and viewpoints that so often have shaped my thinking.
- To Joan Bybee, Oesten Dahl, Larry Gorbet, Umberto Eco, Patrizia Violi, Christina Hellman, Liliane Tasmowski-de Ryck, Sherman Wilcox, Jean-Pierre Koenig, and Tanya Reinhart, who have offered me outstanding opportunities to present and discuss this research publicly.
- To the Cognitive Science and Linguistics communities at UCSD, for their stimulating atmosphere and productive interactions over the past few years, with special thanks to Jean Mandler, Adele Goldberg, Marta Kutas, Adrian Robert, and Rick Grush.
- To Julia Hough of Cambridge University Press for invaluable editorial assistance, help, and encouragement, and to Barbara Folsom and Eric Newman for excellent editing.

Chapter 1
Mappings

This book explores a simple idea: that mappings[1] between domains
are at the heart of the unique human cognitive faculty of producing,
transferring, and processing meaning.

Although simple, this idea is powerful in two ways. It yields general
procedures and principles for a wide array of meaning and reasoning
phenomena, including conceptual projection, conceptual integration and
blending, analogy, reference, and counterfactuals; and it provides us with
insights about the organization of cognitive domains to which we have
no direct access.

This book deals with the evidence for mappings and underlying domains offered by language structure and use. It is meant to be part of
a more general cognitive enterprise that takes into account cultural and
sociological models, learning, psychological development, and neurobiological mappings.

Throughout this study *meaning construction* refers to the high-level,
complex mental operations that apply within and across domains when
we think, act, or communicate. The domains are also mental, and they
include background cognitive and conceptual models as well as locally
introduced mental spaces, which have only partial structure. It has been
a major goal of cognitive linguistics to specify meaning construction,
its operations, its domains, and how they are reflected in language. Research on these matters is progressing rapidly, uncovering the intricate
schemas behind everyday grammar, the richness of underlying conceptual systems, and the complexity of mental space configurations in ordinary discourse.[2] A recurrent finding has been that visible language is
only the tip of the iceberg of invisible meaning construction that goes
on as we think and talk. This hidden, backstage cognition defines our

1. A mapping, in the most general mathematical sense, is a correspondence between two sets that
assigns to each element in the first a counterpart in the second.
2. See, for example, Lakoff (1987), Fauconnier and Sweetser (1996), Langacker (1987, 1991).
Mandler (forthcoming) gives an overview of the notion of representation and the issues relating
to concept formation.

mental and social life. Language is one of its prominent external manifestations.

Meaning construction is a cornerstone of cognitive science. This section briefly reviews some of the reasons why and outlines goals, assumptions, and findings of the new approaches.

1. The Importance and Relevance of Meaning Construction

Scientific inquiry typically starts with the outside world—the stars, the
planets, the elements—before extending to the human world—the body,
the brain, the mind, society. In the development of science as we know it,
physics and chemistry preceded biology, which itself is more advanced
from a technical and operational point of view than, say, cognitive science or sociology.[3] The paradox that we know more about faraway
galaxies than we do about the core of our own planet has a cognitive
analogue: We seem to know a good deal more about the world around
us than we do about our minds and brains.

Science proceeds indirectly; it correlates surface phenomena by interpreting them in certain ways at the observational level and hypoth-
esizing deeper, and more general, relations and principles underlying
the phenomena.[4] Our knowledge of the universe is indirect in just this
way: We infer a rich and complex structure on the basis of very partial
and impoverished data (e.g., signals obtained with some hardship and
considerable technical sophistication). Cognitive science is no different.
Although brains are physically close and accessible, most of what we
can guess about their organization, at the fundamental neurobiological
level, or at somewhat more abstract levels of cognition, is apprehended
indirectly, by observing various kinds of input and output.

In the case of the human mind/brain, one type of signal is especially
pervasive and freely accessible, and that is language. Because we know
language to be intimately connected to some important mental processes,

3. I have in mind here narrow criteria for science as a socially operational and agreed-upon collection
of practices and procedures. There is no value judgment attached to this characterization; modern
sociology, for instance, may well have come up with as many valuable insights as physics without
being at the same stage of science development in the narrow sense.
4. Of course, observation and theory are part of the same overall package; a "phenomenon" requires
a theory, even if it is a folk theory, in order to be observed at all. There is no absolute, direct,
theory-independent observational interpretation of the "facts." As a science evolves, there is
simultaneous, parallel evolution of the observational procedures and interpretations, and of the
explanatory theory itself.

we have in principle a rich, virtually inexhaustible source of data to investigate some aspects of mental processes. So, we must apply our scientific imagination and rational deduction to language signals in the same way that astrophysicists exploit the information they glean from infrared radiation or gamma rays.

But there is a hitch. In studying supernovas or neutrinos, the phenomena, the theories, and our reflections on them are kept apart with relative ease.[5] For language and thought this is not the case: We produce our account of the phenomena under study by using language and thought, that is, by relying on the very phenomenon we are studying. And to make matters worse, the stars and the telescope are confounded: Can language and thought be the instruments for analyzing themselves? The twist of this particular scientific endeavor is that, as human beings immersed in everyday life, we have a rich array of notions (folk-theoretic, one might say) about what we say and what we think, which although in one sense are quite useful, are also in another sense quite wrong and will easily get in the way of our scientific investigation.

Another scientific challenge is to make apparent the extraordinary mystery of language. I have compared language signals coming from the mind/brain to signals received from distant galaxies, or from infinitesimal atoms, that would enable us to make conjectures as to the hidden structures and organizational principles that we cannot apprehend directly. In the case of physics, such signals are typically obtained by means of advanced technology. In today's world, people with no particular interest in astrophysics or quantum mechanics recognize this kind of observation as a significant accomplishment. The fact that we non-specialists do not understand the techniques in detail, or at all, actually adds to the mystery and (correctly) strengthens our sense that something deep is going on. Brain scanners, which light up multicolored screens, are equally impressive. The same cannot be said of language signals: There is a steady flow of talk in the world, and it looks very easily available indeed. What is more, people who study language signals happen, because they are human, to come biologically endowed with very good technology for receiving and processing such signals. But this technical prowess will not immediately impress other human beings,

---

5. At least, this appeared to be the case in physics for a long time; and thinking it was the case was a condition of success. Twentieth-century science cast some doubts on such assumptions, both within the theories themselves (the most notorious but not the only case being Heisenberg's uncertainty principle) and on epistemological grounds (cf. Kuhn 1962).

who are equally gifted for this particular technology and are admirably equipped to use the received signals to produce rich mental constructions with such ease that the entire process does not seem to them especially complicated or mysterious.

I take it, then, that although language data, a richly structured signal emanating from the mind/brain, is in plentiful supply, it is often underestimated scientifically and socially as a source of deeper insight into the human mind.

But isn't such a claim farfetched? Language, after all, has received considerable attention from grammarians, rhetoricians, linguists, philosophers, psychologists, legal scholars, communication experts, and many others. There has been great progress in understanding its structural complexity, in tracking down its semantic and pragmatic subtleties, and in linking its manifestations to other forms of human behavior.

This is true, but if language data is a signal operating on less accessible cognitive constructions, then it is fair to say that linguistic research has focused on the structure of the signal itself rather than on the nonlinguistic constructions to which the signal is connected.[6] Which is fine, as far as it goes: The signal must be understood if we wish to use it inductively to infer its domain of application. But it is equally true that, even if one is only interested in the signal itself, the domain of application and the signal's function are crucially relevant. And it is also fair to say that nonlinguistic research has paid little attention to the basic nature of meaning constructions and their subtle and principled links to syntactic form.

Modern linguistics, structuralist or generative, has treated language as an autonomous object of study. It has not been concerned with using language data within the larger project envisioned here: gaining access to the rich meaning constructions upon which language operates.

In philosophy, on the other hand, there has been awareness that language organization could reveal more than its own structural principles, and many interesting issues have been raised. Many of us find the problems fascinating yet remain disappointed by the results. We think that the range of data examined is insufficient and improperly selected, and that the range of interesting hypotheses is usually severely constrained by a priori theoretical assumptions, which receive little explicit

6. There are more and more exceptions nowadays to this dominating tendency, especially in recent cognitively oriented work.

attention. We see this as a source of circularity, as the assumptions in question are in fact in themselves an important target of the investigation.

A related shortcoming of modern work, found in this case both in linguistics and in philosophy, is the sharp emphasis on separating components (e.g., syntactic, semantic, pragmatic) and attempting to study the grammatical or meaning structure of expressions independently of their function in building up discourse, and independently of their use in reasoning and communication. In fact, discourse configurations are highly organized and complex within wider social and cultural contexts, and the raison d'être of grammatical constructions and words within them is to provide us with (imperfect) clues as to what discourse configurations to set up. A major finding of cognitive semantics and mental-space research is that the same mapping operations and principles are at work in elementary semantics, pragmatics, and so-called higher-level reasoning. The analysis of tense, reference, presupposition, and counterfactuals is intimately tied to that of analogical mappings, conceptual connections, and discourse construction, which in turn is inseparable from the understanding of metaphor and metonymy, narrative structure, speech acts, rhetoric, and general reasoning.

2. Goals and Techniques

2.1. Structures and Data

Why is meaning construction an important field of inquiry, and why should we hope to have better luck with it now than in the past? I suggested above, with respect to the first question, that in spite of much language-related research, language data remained underestimated and underexploited as a unique and amazing source of information for reconstructing deeper cognitive processes. But this broad observation remains useless unless we come up with a positive answer to the second question. Are we today in a better position to use available data (the language "signals") for the purpose of discovering inferentially some of the hidden cognitive processes at work? Let us look at some signs of hope.

First, the level of scientific sophistication in modern linguistics is impressive. To quote the philosopher Hilary Putnam: "Language is the first broad area of human cognitive capacity for which we are beginning to obtain a description which is not exaggeratedly oversimplified. Thanks to the work of contemporary transformational linguists, a very subtle description of at least some human languages is in the process of being constructed."[7]

This is perhaps most evident in phonology, where very abstract and elegant theories are emerging. In syntax and areas of semantics and pragmatics the field is more disparate, but the scientific methodology is there, even if the foundations are still shaky. Huge amounts of data are submitted to intensive investigation, abstract universal principles of explanation are sought for in the best scientific tradition, and sophisticated argumentation strategies are marshalled in support of theoretical standpoints. As was pointed out in the previous section, this excellent scientific methodology is for the time being very strongly directed at the internal structure of language viewed as an autonomous object of inquiry, rather than at the richer cognitive constructions that language use helps to target. There is no reason why the same rigor, thoroughness, and imaginative invention should not be applied to the broader issue.[8]

This is already the case in many respects. Theoretical research on language has followed a curious path in the last twenty years. The emphasis on studying structure for its own sake and independently of meaning and use, inherited from twentieth-century structuralism, was preserved in principle within the transformational, generative, or relational approaches; but, oddly enough, this structuralist dogma opened the door to wide-scale research in semantics and pragmatics. The reason is this. Luckily for those of us interested in meaning, the strong version of the autonomy of linguistic form happens to be wrong for natural language; judgments of grammaticality and acceptability are dependent to various degrees on many features linked to context, meaning, and use. This im-

---

7. Putnam 1975.
8. This optimistic statement is misleading. There are certainly no reasons having to do with the subject matter or the scientific goals. But there may exist some contingent obstacles; there is a strong and perfectly defensible tradition among linguists and grammarians to reify language, to study what Saussure called "langue" independently of "parole." Although this insistence on keeping the study of language pure by isolating it from everything else has indeed led to success in many instances, it turns out to be much too strong a requirement, even when our goals are limited to understanding language phenomena. Another contingent obstacle is the difficulty for other cognitive scientists without training in linguistics to understand the complexity and deceptiveness of issues pertaining to natural language. Again, I imply no criticism; it unfortunately takes years and years for many of us to shed our natural everyday prejudices about language (if in fact we ever do); and this is presumably because language and thought are such an intimate and direct component of our existence—something we do so well and so easily—that we have trouble realizing how little we understand it.

portant property of natural language has had a simple consequence for research founded on the structuralist approach: As linguists advanced further and further in their study of form, they kept stumbling more and more often on questions of meaning. There were two types of responses to this epistemological quandary. One was to narrow the scope of syntax so as to exclude, if possible, the troublesome phenomena from the primary data.[9] The other was to widen the scope of inquiry so that issues of form and of meaning could be encompassed simultaneously.[10] But it was now clear, in any event, that the time had come to break away from a science of language centered exclusively on syntax and phonology; it was urgent to concentrate on the difficult problem of meaning construction.

But is this problem a scientifically tractable one? The structuralists didn't think so; and they were right, given the restrictions they had placed on available data: There is no hope of retrieving interesting principles of meaning organization from surface distributions alone.[11] Fortunately, we need not limit ourselves to the very restrictive data of the structuralist tradition (distributions of words in an attested corpus), or of the generative tradition (native-speaker intuitions as to the well-formedness of strings of words, independent of context, local situations, or cultural assumptions). We have access to much richer and perfectly legitimate sources of data: first, knowledge of the circumstances in which language productions occurred and knowledge of some of the inferences that participants were able to make on the basis of such productions; second, speaker intuitions about possible understandings of expressions in various settings. To be sure, no one claims that it is straightforward to obtain such data. But this is hardly a reason to spurn it; the natural sciences devote much of their energy to devising ways of gathering data that is not readily accessible. Cognitive science successfully takes into account cultural and situational data as well as computational and biological data.[12]

To put things a little differently, language data suffers when it is restricted to language, for the simple reason that the interesting cognitive constructions underlying language use have to do with complete

9. This was the course followed in particular by Noam Chomsky and his students from 1971 on. Efforts were concentrated on a core syntax covering few language phenomena.
10. Many studies, especially during the 1970s, showed how certain aspects of syntactic distribution were conditioned in part by pragmatic conditions. See, for example, Ross 1970, Sadock 1974, Fauconnier 1975.
11. Zellig Harris (1951, 1952) gave it his best shot.
12. Sociolinguistics is, of course, an important field dealing insightfully with some situated aspects of language. My remarks in the text concern core theories of meaning and form.

situations that include highly structured background knowledge, various kinds of reasoning, on-line meaning construction, and negotiation of meaning.[13] And, for the same reason, language theory suffers when it is restricted to language.

Now all of the above might be right and still irrelevant in practice if we had no idea how to carry out the research program it suggests. And indeed, there has been a good deal of pessimism regarding such programs over the years: There were formalisms at hand for grammar (exported from computability theory) and for truth-conditional semantics (exported from logic); and there was a plethora of informal ideas about meaning in context, the structure of discourse and conversation, and so on. None of this seemed likely to achieve the kind of goals mentioned here—uncovering principles of cognitive construction behind language use. In fact, some philosophers became so wary of mental representations that they preferred to regard language expressions as referring directly to actual and possible worlds. We now have a pretty good idea of why this approach did not work out: When language expressions reflect objective events and situations, as they often do (and often do not), they do not reflect them directly, but rather through elaborate human cognitive constructions and construals.

What is exciting today is that we are starting to catch a glimpse of what such constructions might be. Philosophical speculation in this domain has yielded to detailed work in anthropology, psychology, cognitive sociology, semantics, and cognitive science more generally. To put it simply, we are beginning to break away from our a priori and everyday life conceptions of how human beings reason, talk, and interact, and to discover some of the models, principles of organization, and biological mechanisms that may actually be at work. What we discover is often surprising and runs counter to "commonsense" beliefs, as well as to highly sophisticated theories.

This brings us back to the topic of this book: mappings between cognitive domains that are set up when we think and when we talk. By and large, such mappings, when acknowledged at all, had been confined to phenomena considered peripheral, such as literary metaphor or analogy. But recently, there has been mounting evidence for the central

---

13. Everyday meaning construction requires on-line creativity (see Chapters 4 and 6). Moreover, meaning constructions (highly underspecified by language) are negotiated by participants in communication. Lois Bloom, back in 1974, and before the advent of cognitive linguistics, stressed that there is no one-to-one relation between linguistic facts and real-world events; language is directed at the internal mental representation of experience.

role played by various kinds of mappings at the very heart of natural language semantics and everyday reasoning.

Projection mappings will project part of the structure of one domain onto another. The case for metaphorical mappings has been made by Reddy (1979), Lakoff and Johnson (1980), Turner (1986, 1991), Lakoff and Turner (1989), Sweetser (1990), Indurkhya (1992), Gibbs (1994), and many others. We shall have more to say later on about such mappings;[14] the general (and deep) idea is that, in order to talk and think about some domains (*target* domains) we use the structure of other domains (*source* domains) and the corresponding vocabulary. Some of these mappings are used by all members of a culture—for instance, in English, TIME AS SPACE. We use structure from our everyday conception of space and motion to organize our everyday conception of time, as when we say: *Christmas is approaching; The weeks go by; Summer is around the corner; The long day stretched out with no end in sight.* Mappings become culturally and lexically entrenched, and as Turner (1991) shows, they actually define the category structure for the language and culture. Rather remarkably, although the vocabulary often makes the mapping transparent, we are typically not conscious of the mapping during use, and in fact are liable to be surprised and amused when it is pointed out to us. In such cases, the mapping, although cognitively active, is opaque: The projection of one domain onto another is in some sense automatic. Domain projection mappings may also be set up locally, in context, in which case they are typically perceived not as belonging to the language, but rather as "creative" and part of the ongoing reasoning and discourse construction. There is, however, no formal difference between the lexically entrenched (opaque) cases and the ones that are consciously perceived as innovative.[15] Many of the latter are in fact simple extensions of the former.

Sweetser (1990) has studied an important case of domain mapping that explains the superficially diverse and logically puzzling uses of modals,

---

14. This chapter, section 2.2.2, and Chapter 6, section 4
15. There has been a strange reluctance on the part of some philosophers to come to grips with the linguistic facts pertaining to projection mappings and their semantic implications (cf., e.g., Davidson 1979). Failing to see the wealth of data supporting the case for synchronic projection mappings, they have tried to reduce the few isolated examples they discussed to remnants of diachronic change ("dead" metaphor). This approach, besides being factually incorrect, also has things backwards theoretically, because diachronic change is just as much in need of explanation as anything else; and, as it turns out, the explanation for semantic change lies in major part on the synchronic projection mappings. Sweetser (forthcoming) gives an excellent analysis of this process for recurring changes in Indo-European vocabularies.

like *may, must,* or *can,* in English. Modals express physical laws of nature, social constraints and permissions, logical necessity and possibility, and conversational organization: *Animals must die; Cinderella must be home before midnight; Guests may park here; Harry must have forgotten his money; Felix may be a professor but he sure is dumb.* Drawing on L. Talmy's work, Sweetser has shown that (at least) three domains—content, epistemic, and speech–act—were matched and structured by force dynamics. Her general account provides an elegant explanation of the apparent polysemy of modals, and shows how inferences are transferred from a concrete domain (content) to an abstract one (epistemic). One aspect of this work is that our conceptualization of reasoning is linked to our conceptualization of space and motion, as is suggested by the use of spatial expressions to talk about reasoning:

> This **leads** to a new theorem. They **reached** a different conclusion. This proof **stands in the way** of your conjecture. Try to think **straight**. This **line** of reasoning is **taking you in the wrong direction.**

Sweetser's account shows how the force dynamics in the content domain of motion is projected onto the epistemic domain of reasoning. A modal like *must* will mean generally that a force is applied, yielding superficially different senses depending on the domain of application (e.g., physical, social, epistemic, esthetic):

Animals must eat to survive.
Cinderella must be back home before midnight.
Nero must have been cruel.
The armchair must go in the left corner of the bedroom.

Lakoff (1987) shows how inference inherently built in a source domain (e.g., containers) will be transferred by projection to an abstract domain (e.g., Boolean logic), and how such mappings will combine to yield different meanings. For example, metaphors of SEEING as TOUCHING and KNOWING as SEEING combine with one sense of *over* to motivate *overlook:* the line of sight travels "over" (i.e., above) the object; hence there is no contact; hence it is not seen; hence it is not noticed or taken into account. In contrast, *look over* ("*she looked over the draft*"), uses a related but different sense of *over*, a path covering much of a surface, as in "*she wandered over the entire field.*" This sense combines with the same mappings to produce a very different meaning—the object in this case is seen and noticed.[16]

16. The complex network of spatial senses of *over* is analyzed by Brugman 1988.

Another important class of domain connections are the *pragmatic function mappings*. Pragmatic functions are studied in Nunberg (1978, 1979). The two relevant domains, which may be set up locally, typically correspond to two categories of objects, which are mapped onto each other by a pragmatic function. For example, authors are matched with the books they write, or hospital patients are matched with the illnesses for which they are being treated. This kind of mapping plays an important role in structuring our knowledge base and provides means of identifying elements of one domain via their counterparts in the other. Pragmatic function mappings, like projection mappings, will often be responsible for semantic change over time. Metonymy and synecdoche are pragmatic function mappings.[17] In language use, pragmatic function mappings allow an entity to be identified in terms of its counterpart in the projection. So, when the nurse says

The gastric ulcer in Room 12 would like some coffee

(s)he is using the illness (the gastric ulcer) to identify the patient who has it.

A third class of mappings, *schema mappings*, operate when a general schema, frame, or model is used to structure a situation in context. In Langacker's cognitive grammar framework (Langacker 1987, 1991), grammatical constructions and vocabulary items "call up" meaning schemas. We can view the elaboration of such schemas by successive steps in the grammatical construction as a set of correspondences between abstract schemas.

As we shall see throughout this book, mappings operate to build and link *mental spaces*. Mental spaces (Fauconnier 1994) are partial structures that proliferate when we think and talk, allowing a fine-grained partitioning of our discourse and knowledge structures. For instance, in saying *Liz thinks Richard is wonderful*, we build a space for Liz's reported beliefs, with minimal explicit structure corresponding to Richard's being wonderful. In saying *Last year, Richard was wonderful*, we build a space for "last year," and in saying *Liz thinks that last year Richard was wonderful*, we build a space for last year embedded in a belief space, itself embedded in a base space. Chapter 2 will examine the notion of mental space in some detail.

Lakoff (1987, chap. 4) mentions that mental spaces are structured by ICMs (idealized cognitive models). Again, this can be viewed as a form

17. Studies in rhetoric usually single out some of the most common pragmatic functions or pragmatic function types and come up with a finite list (a dozen or so) of typical metonymies.

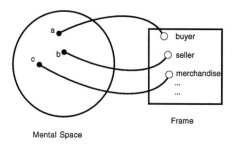

Figure 1.1.

of schematic mapping. Take, for instance, the case where the ICM is a frame, as in Fillmore (1982, 1985), for example, the frame for "buying and selling," with a buyer, a seller, merchandise, currency, price,[18] and a rich set of inferences pertaining to ownership, commitments, exchange, and so on. If a sentence like *Jack buys gold from Jill* occurs in the discourse, and if *Jack, Jill, gold,* identify elements *a, b, c,* in a mental space, then those elements will be mapped onto the appropriate slots in the "buying and selling" frame (Fig. 1.1).

This is also the approach taken by Hofstadter, Clossman, and Meredith (1982). Definite descriptions like "the seller" identify *roles* in the appropriate frame. In a simple example like the one above, the mapping between space and frame is straightforward. We shall see later on how the power of mappings is exploited in such cases to yield accounts of more complex phenomena. In particular, we shall see how roles are set up as elements in the spaces themselves and are connected to ICMs that serve as default models, and also how frames can be constructed locally within spaces, rather than just extracted from background knowledge.

The mappings alluded to—projection mappings, pragmatic function mappings, and schematic mappings—are central to any understanding of semantic and pragmatic language interpretation and cognitive construction. Once we start looking for them, mappings show up in large numbers and in unexpected places. I will be concerned in particular with *mental-space mappings*, which link mental spaces set up in discourse and account for logically puzzling properties of various types of phenomena such as counterfactuals, hypotheticals, quantification, atemporal *when*, narrative tenses and deictics, indirect and direct discourse.

18. Frames of this kind can be very schematic or more specific, depending on how far we delve into our knowledge base to take into account contextual specifications.

If mappings, as claimed above, are so central to meaning construction, one wonders why they have been all but ignored by grammarians, logicians, and philosophers. After all, mappings are at the very foundation of mathematics and structure many scientific theories. Their importance has been acknowledged in cognitive psychology, as by Norman (1988), and in cognitive anthropology (Hutchins 1995). What is more, recent work in neurobiology (Sereno 1991b; Churchland 1986; Edelman 1992; Damasio 1994) has stressed the importance of physically instantiated mappings and connections between areas of the brain.[19]

Why, then, have mappings been overlooked? The answer may be simple: In order for mappings to come into play, there have to be domains to map onto each other. Modern mathematics, which starts out with sets, has the appropriate domains right away; but it took many centuries for mathematics to come upon this fundamental unifying concept, and set theory was the key to unification.

In the case of language, the domains that we need in order to understand language functioning are not in the combinatorial structure of language itself; they are in the cognitive constructions that language acts upon. As long as language is studied as an autonomous self-contained structure, such domains will be invisible. We may have suffered here from a modern epistemological paradox: In studying natural languages autonomously, it is reasonable to treat them formally as sets of strings. And in so doing, one appeals to a branch of mathematics where mappings are not all that important: the theory of formal languages and rewriting systems. Paradoxically, modern linguistics, with its overriding emphasis on syntax, got itself connected to a mathematics without mappings, exactly the sort that will not help us for the study of meaning.[20]

2.2. Some Examples

This section takes an informal look at a number of cases where it is fairly transparent that mappings between domains are operating. General characteristics of the data and issues will be pointed out. In the next chapter, major aspects of the mental space framework will be outlined, so that we can tackle the general issue of mappings in language in a precise and comprehensive manner. My goal at this point is to survey the issue in a nontechnical way, and show some of its hidden complexities.

19. Edelman's book stresses the important mutual challenge for neurobiology and cognitive linguistics to account for each other's findings.
20. Phonology broke away earlier from the purely combinatorial perspective: Mappings between levels have become a powerful theoretical concept.

2.2.1. Counterfactuals

Consider the following example offered by Charles Fillmore. Suppose it is said by an angry baby-sitter talking to a rebellious child.

If I were your father, I would spank you.

Examples like this are called counterfactuals, because they set up, alongside a presupposed reality ("I am not your father, I am not spanking you"), an imagined situation counter to fact ("I am your father, I spank you"). Counterfactual expressions are not just fanciful flights of the imagination; they are meant to have actual impact on reality and the shaping of real events. How can this be? What kind of inferences are produced? How are they produced?

First, as Fillmore notes, there is more than one way to build up the counterfactual meaning, and different choices can lead to dramatically different consequences. Here are some of the possibilities for our example:

(1) The Lenient Father Interpretation. The baby-sitter, whom we shall call Sue, believes that the father (Harry) should show more authority. She is suggesting that the father might be well-advised to spank this child (Tom). How can the imaginary counterfactual convey this? Certainly, Sue is not considering a world in which she is the biological father of Tom. Rather, she is constructing a situation in which the father's dispositions (leniency, weakness) are replaced by different dispositions, presented as her own (severity, authority). Why would this entail any criticism of the father or suggest that he modify his behavior? An added pragmatic default principle is needed: P_1 (egocentric attribution)—The speaker's behavior and dispositions in an imaginary situation are construed as desirable. P_1 is behind the common use of counterfactuals to give advice:

In your place, I would resign.
If it were me, I wouldn't put up with it.
If I were you, I wouldn't mess with me.

But P_1 is by no means obligatory. Sue may be commenting as before on what her dispositions would lead her to do (spank Tom), but mean it as a positive comment on the father's self-restraint or as a negative comment on her own impulsivity.

Common to these superficially diverging interpretations is the type of correspondence established between the real and imaginary situations. The two are mapped onto each other. The mapping is *identity* in most respects (Tom remains Tom, and remains obnoxious, the setting for Tom's behavior is unchanged, etc.), but Sue is mapped onto Harry, the father, with respect to relevant (but not explicitly specified) dispositions, whereas Harry is mapped onto Harry in other respects (being the father, having a beard, etc.). Only very partial structure is manipulated: There is no attempt to examine what other effects the Sue-for-Harry substitution might have, because the goal is to build a real-world inference (that the father is too lenient or admirably patient), not to explore the imaginary world in which he shares some of Sue's characteristics.

Furthermore, at the same time that the mapping is counterfactually linking Sue and Harry, it can project Sue independently as Sue into the counterfactual:

If I were your father, I would pay my baby-sitter better.

In the imaginary situation, Harry (with Sue's desirable dispositions) gives Sue a raise. The double link is similar in the example *If I were you, I wouldn't mess with me.*

(2) The Stern Father Reading. Sue can be understood to be saying something quite different. She is pointing out to the child, Tom, how stern the father is and how lenient she is in comparison. This amounts to telling Tom how lucky he is (given his outrageous behavior) that it is Sue and not Harry who is in charge: Sue will not spank him, but Harry would.

The grammatical form of the sentence is of course the same as before, and Sue (in reality) is still being mapped onto Harry (in the imaginary situation invoked). But this time it is not Sue's dispositions that get transferred. Rather, it is the father, with all of his real properties including dispositions, who physically takes Sue's place in the local situation.

Of course, the inference that Tom deserves a spanking might again be derived under this form of the mapping, but through a totally different route. What we see is that the grammatical form of the sentence (*if X were Y . . .*) invites the understander to find a counterfactual mapping from Sue in reality to an imaginary Harry, but does not fully specify what gets transferred. The imaginary situation impacts on reality by expanding the understander's construal of what is going on: For example, the fact that the father would act in a certain way in Sue's place puts Tom's action in a familiar context where it is more obvious that it is bad, that he should stop doing it, and perhaps should worry about his father being told about it. Finally, pragmatic defaults like P_1 may operate, so that Sue is understood to be pointing out how nice *she* is, or how lucky *both* of them are that Harry is away.

The theoretical import of all this is that grammar guides the meaning construction up to a point, and that further choices need to be made at the construction level (specifics of the mapping) and at the pragmatics level (relevant implications of the counterfactual).

(3) The Role Reading.   There is yet another way to construct a meaning for Fillmore's example without bringing in Harry at all, or even supposing that Tom has a father. We can take Sue to be saying that, if she had the social attributes of fatherhood, then she would spank Tom. The counterfactual in that case maps Sue onto Sue, but the imaginary Sue, as opposed to the real one, is the father of Tom. Interestingly, from a logical point of view, the objective factors that prevent Sue from actually being the father (she's a woman, she's unrelated to Tom, she's too young, etc.) do not preclude the construction. Again, this is because the point of the counterfactual in this context is to highlight the disanalogy between Susan's actual role and other conceivable social situations; the point is not to examine the possibility of Susan being Tom's biological father.

But of course it *could* be. Suppose the speaker is not Sue but Robert, and that there is some uncertainty as to who Tom's father is. The same sentence, with the role reading, could be used to argue that Robert is not the father.

In sum, our informal observation of Fillmore's example suggests the following aspects of meaning construction:

- The grammatical form of the sentence prompts us to look for a mapping from a very partial aspect of the real situation onto a counterfactual one. In the minimum configuration we considered, there are three mappings that will meet the grammatically specified conditions.[21]
- Each of these mappings may in turn be pragmatically exploited in different ways, so that a larger number of truth-conditionally distinct elaborated meanings are derivable—criticism versus praise of Harry, criticism of Tom, self-praise of Sue, self-deprecation, complaint, implication that the speaker is not the father, and so on.

---

21. In a richer discourse configuration, there would be more (see Chapter 5). The number of available mappings is not a simple structural property of the expression.

Clearly, if we really want to know how language helps to create full meanings, and how the grammar links up to the interpretation, we need to take all this into account. We also need to study the mapping possibilities directly, because there is no single logical form that we could associate with our sentence, and that would then yield all the interpretations considered, through pragmatic elaboration.

A major focus of this book will be to find out how the mappings operate, and what they operate on. This goal is apparently more ambitious than the traditional one of specifying a semantic representation for sentences in isolation, but we will show that it is in fact more realistic, because there is no such thing as an isolated meaning representation. The language, it will be argued, does not autonomously specify meanings that later undergo pragmatic processing. Rather, it guides meaning construction directly in context.

Now look at another counterfactual that will be studied in detail later.

In France, Watergate would not have harmed Nixon.

As in the previous case, there are many interpretations for this form. Consider the one intended to make a general point about the French political system, something like: A French president in Nixon's circumstances, and with some of his attributes, would not be harmed (in the way that Nixon was) by a political incident similar to Watergate. How can such a reading arise? Clearly not from building up the almost impossible world in which Nixon is actually the French head of state, and Watergate is really in France. Even less from scenarios where Nixon moves to France in order to avoid the unpleasantness of the Watergate scandal. Rather, the simple example sentence is setting up a complex disanalogy. Its operation requires, first, an elementary analogy between similar political systems, the French and the American—both have presidents, voters, public opinion, occasional scandals, and so on. They can therefore be partially mapped onto each other. Our example sentence is exploiting this analogy to effect a further partial mapping of the two initial domains (French and American) onto a third *counterfactual* one. The third domain shares the common structure of the first two: president, voters, and so on. It inherits from "France" the majority of its background properties; it inherits from "U.S.A." relevant properties of the Watergate scandal and President Nixon, but as they are not (and presumably cannot be) explicitly specified, there is some latitude in actually pinning them down. The third domain is counterfactual, because there is no reference to an actual scandal in France, but it produces real inferences back to the initial domains, in the form of a disanalogy: Given the structural analogy of the two political systems, there could be, and perhaps will be, or have been, Watergate-like incidents in France; but such incidents would not have the same effects as they had in the actual U.S. case. Notice how this comment, although based on a counterfactual, is quite informative, for it presents a law-like generalization about France and makes predictions about past and future events.

2.2.2. Analogy, Metaphor, and Conceptual Systems

Our conceptual networks are intricately structured by analogical and metaphorical mappings, which play a key role in the synchronic construction of meaning and in its diachronic evolution. Parts of such mappings are so entrenched in everyday thought and language that we do not consciously notice them; other parts strike us as novel and creative. The term *metaphor* is often applied to the latter, highlighting the literary and poetic aspects of the phenomenon. But the general cognitive principles at work are the same, and they play a key role in thought and language at all levels.

Consider the recent emergence of the notion "computer virus." It is manifested linguistically in expressions like the following:

Viruses are programs developed by renegade computer operators who covertly implant them in other programs.
Infections can spread from computer to computer as fast as the Hong Kong flu.
Files are contaminated by infectious bytes.
Compuserve can never be completely immune to hidden killers.
Data physicians develop vaccines, disinfectants, . . .
The only way users can be assured that their programs are healthy is through safe interface.

We can all see that vocabulary from the domain of health, biology, and medicine is being used to talk and reason about the domain of computers and programming. Viruses have been mapped onto undesirable, harmful programs, which replicate themselves, erase files, and so on. Vaccines are mapped onto programs that counter the first; physicians map onto computer technicians, attempting to block the action of the harmful programs, and so on.

The example is in many ways straightforward. And it is readily assimilated by speakers of the language long before dictionaries and manuals formally record the new meanings that arise. Yet the process is cognitively complex and consists of several nontrivial stages and transitions typical of what goes on in all other areas of our conceptual systems. Here are some aspects of the evolution of such a conceptual system under pressure from analogy, metaphor, the real world, and other already available mappings and generic frames.

(1) Analogy and Schema Induction. We are able to recognize generic-level features of biological viruses that are independent of their biological nature but follow from the way we conceptualize them and relate them to other aspects of our lives. For instance:

- x is present, but unwanted; it comes in, or is put in, from the outside; it does not naturally belong;
- x is able to replicate; new tokens of x appear that have the same undesirable properties as the original x;
- x disrupts the "standard" function of the system;
- x is harmful to the system, and hence is harmful to users of the system.
- the system should be protected against x; this might be achieved if the system were such that x could not come into it, or if other elements were added to the system that would counteract the effects of x, or eject x, or destroy x.

This is not just a list of properties; it is an integrated schema, supported by elementary image schemas, such as "container" and "path," force dynamics (x tries to get in, the system and its users try to block it), causal schemas (abstract goals of x, of users), and so on. A good part of the schema has widespread application in social life: keeping allegedly harmful intruders out of established groups, worms out of apples, spies out of the military, the Trojan horse out of Troy. . . .

The very partial structure of the health domain relative to viruses is not just a random case of the schema. It is, in Langacker's terms, an archetype: an exceptionally good and readily accessible representative of the abstract schema. It is also one that elaborates the more general intruder schema with some precision: x is hard to spot, x self-replicates. Because the elaborated schema fits the generic aspects of the computer situation, the analogy is successful: the harmful programs also self-replicate, are hard to discern, demand countermeasures, and so on. Preexisting functional analogies between machines and living organisms favor the new mapping—computers respond to commands, play tricks on us, have memories.

As students of analogy often point out, the similarity between domains that gets exploited here is one of structure, not of substance. We do not, at least in the first stages, use *virus* or *vaccine* with any implication that the computer actually has biological properties or substance. The *induced schema* that sanctions the analogy is at a very high level of abstraction. It ignores the technical aspects of each domain. And, in fact, this makes it accessible to language users who have no knowledge of medicine or computer science. Such users—by far the majority—rely on experts to extract the nontechnical generic-level properties of biological viruses and computer programs. Their understanding of the input domains is itself limited to highly schematic and nontechnical interfaces: when the physician tells me that a virus is in my body and that penicillin will act against it, I need have only a highly metaphorical interpretation of the complex biological process to which she is alluding.

Analogical mapping is so commonplace that we take it for granted. But it is one of the great mysteries of cognition. Given the richness of the domains and their complexity, how are the "right" schemas consistently extracted, elaborated, and applied to further mappings? And what are these schemas and generic frames that structure our conceptual systems so pervasively?

(2) Categorization and New Conceptual Structure. In a second stage, analogy develops into categorization of the target domain. We can now assign certain programs to the category "virus," others to the categories "vaccine" or "disinfectant." Computer technicians specialized in detecting and blocking the harmful programs form a novel category ("data physicians").

It is important to realize that the mapping is a way of thinking about aspects of the target domain and of acting upon it. It is not directly a reflection of a preexisting objective structure of that domain. We can start looking for "disinfectants" and "vaccines," we can think of making our system "immune" or "safe" before we know if this is technologically feasible, and a fortiori before the computer domain actually contains any real equivalents of "disinfectants" or "immunity." In this kind of case, we are not just conceptualizing an already given domain in a certain way, we are actually building it so that it fits the mapping; the technicians and inventors are finding programs, counterprograms, blocking devices that will fit the generic conceptual specifications of the health/computer analogy.

Of course, there might be no real instantiation of this conceptualization: reality might stand in the way of building a domain that would meet the conditions abstractly specified by the mapping. Then, the adopted categorization might break down simply because "it doesn't work." Interestingly, in the case of computer viruses, it goes through: the conceptualization is viable and guides the technical work with some success. But note once more the high-level schematic nature of the mapping; at a lower level, the technicians will no longer be using the biological analogy—they will be relying on domain-specific knowledge about computers.

Language reflects to some degree the presence of analogical categorization and conceptualization by allowing the vocabulary of a source domain to apply to counterparts in the target. We don't just say that the harmful program is "like" a virus. We go ahead and *call* it a virus. In all the examples cited above, health vocabulary is directly applied to the target domain of computers (*infections, spread, contaminated, immune, healthy*). Later we shall examine two deep reasons for the existence of such transfer, mental-space access, and space blending, but for the time being it is sufficient to view transfer descriptively. When a mapping is in the first two stages we consider here, the vocabulary transfer is subjectively felt to be "metaphorical": programs are not really viruses; a machine is not really healthy or contaminated. The metaphorical vocabulary highlights the role of the source domain in providing conceptual categorization for the target. But this leads to a third stage of the process.

(3) Naming and Projected Structure.   With the mapping in place and vocabulary transfer operating, the target finds itself named and structured. Expressions like *virus, protection, and disinfectant* can be viewed as applying directly to the new conceptual categories of the target domain. This does not sever the link between the original source domain and the target or diminish the importance of the source as an archetype for some abstract properties of the target; but it does modify our synchronic conception of the vocabulary itself. We no longer feel ourselves to be talking about certain programs "as if" they were viruses; rather, our subjective and not very conscious impression is that we are now using the term *virus*

to speak of such programs. This aspect of naming is often misunderstood and leads to needless controversy. In many accounts of meaning, the incorrect interpretation of the phenomenon is that the metaphor is now dead and that words such as *virus* have acquired new meanings. In fact, quite the opposite is the case. The analogical mapping is not only alive, it is now entrenched in the conceptual and grammatical system. What the entrenchment does is make the mapping less noticeable at a conscious level; but at another level, it is more available than ever for reasoning, inference transfers, and conceptual elaborations. In a sense that will be made precise in Chapters 2, 4, and 6, the conceptual network has been extended by the analogical mapping and the vocabulary finds itself simultaneously associated with mapped counterparts. This enables us to think directly of *computer viruses* without consciously activating the source biological domain, and yet to use the relevant conceptual properties of that domain, because they are now projected inherently onto the target and linked to the generic, more abstract, induction schema that motivated the analogy in the first place. At the same time, *virus*, when used in the computer domain, is now endowed with additional more specific attributes not in the source or in the induction schema. In that sense, we do have an evolution of meaning: as we construct and understand our target domain in finer detail, the term *virus* in that domain will come to be associated with many features that were not present at the outset in any of the inputs (source, target, induced schema). And such features will usually be absent from the source and specific to the target. From that point on, several scenarios can occur: blending, motivated polysemy, or divergence.

(4) Blending and Conceptual Integration.   Blending, a cognitive operation introduced in Fauconnier and Turner (1994), will be examined in some detail in Chapter 6. Informally, it consists in integrating partial structures from two separate domains into a single structure with emergent properties within a third domain. In the virus example, it works like this: once the mapping between health and computers is in place, with common vocabulary applying to mapped counterparts, it is possible to blend the two notions of *virus* (biological and computational) into a third integrated notion that incorporates the first two and goes beyond them. This amounts to a formation of novel categories denoted by single terms. In the extended domain that we build, the term *virus* covers a category containing both the biological organisms and the harmful programs. They are now conceived to be "the same

kind of thing," not just counterparts in an analogy or domain-specific instances of an abstract schema. In the blend, then, there is a virus category, of which the biological viruses and the computer viruses are two subcategories. Members of the new category are not restricted to members of the input domains (health and computers). The blend opens up a possible search for members in other domains—for instance, social viruses or mental viruses (destructive ideas that propagate, mutate, and replicate).

Note that the generic induction schema is usually insufficient to define what will fall into the blend. It is too skeletal and abstract. The blend, on the contrary, is typically richer than its input structures: it elaborates a category in many directions, containing specific instances and the fine details that go with them.

When a blend gains consistence, it reorganizes our categories and allows thought to move in new directions. There is evidence that the computer virus conceptualization has moved in this way for some of us. As reported by the *New York Times*, J. Doyne Farmer, a researcher at Los Alamos National Laboratory, writes: "Although computer viruses are not fully alive, they embody many of the characteristics of life, and it is not hard to imagine computer viruses of the future that will be just as alive as biological viruses."

Of interest here, of course, is the integration of the two virus counterparts into a single blended category, and also the introduction of new issues: What is it to be "alive," "fully alive," beyond the confines of biology? The question would not have made sense at an earlier stage of the conceptual evolution, when the notion of "alive" was not one transferred from the biological to the computational domain. It is also worth noting that Farmer writes in the context of research on "artificial life." In this research, the direction of the analogical mapping linking biology and computation has been reversed: What comes under scrutiny are the computational properties of biological evolution and the simulation by genetic algorithms of evolutionary phenomena. We thus have mappings in both directions, and this clearly facilitates the blending integration process. If successful, such a blend would support a novel science in which artificial and biological life are no longer fundamentally distinguished.

Also relevant are the deeply entrenched metaphors of life in everyday talk: a battery is dead, a theory is alive and well, ideas are born, die, resurrect, and so on. At the highest level, motion is life (analogically); immobility, disappearance, inability to function, are death.

(5) Motivated Polysemy.   Instead of blending together, the two domains
in correspondence may stay apart, and even become increasingly distinguished, but without losing their analogical and linguistic links. In
the virus example, this happens when terms like *virus* and *disinfectant* are applied so automatically to the target domain that they are
no longer felt to be analogical or metaphorical. At one level of use,
a feeling of polysemy is produced. The word *virus* means two different things: the microbe and the sneaky program. At a less conscious
level, however, the biological and computational networks of meaning
remain linked. The source domain of health and biology remains "in
the wings" and can be used at any time to provide further vocabulary
and, more important, new ideas for dealing with the target. One reads of
computer viruses infecting new machines and *lying dormant* for weeks,
and of the urgency of establishing centers for *disease control* for computer viruses. This is not just a manner of speaking. Just as the AIDS
virus is foremost in our minds, so there is genuine fear among computer scientists that artificial viruses may get out of control and spread
to countrywide networks, with catastrophic economic consequences.
In trying to deal with such dangers, scientists once again export conceptual information from the biological source. The newspaper article
quoted earlier reports that, according to some specialists, the answer is
to adopt more heterogeneous software: "more diverse software would
make it difficult for computer viruses to spread widely, just as the di-
versity of biological life keeps a single invader from wiping out entire
populations."

(6) Divergence and Extinction.   Real divergence between domains occurs when the vocabulary remains but the conceptual links disappear,
or when a source domain changes its vocabulary while the target keeps
the original vocabulary, so that the mapping is no longer linguistically
transparent. The latter change is a widespread and recurring feature of
language evolution. As Sweetser (1990) emphasizes, conceptual mappings linking vision, manipulation, and knowledge are found over and
over again in languages. In modern English, *grasp* retains the senses of
seizing and understanding, *see* applies to vision and to intellection; we
can *catch* a prey, *catch* sight of a comet, *catch* the meaning of a joke. But
many words become specialized for use in one or the other of the linked
domains: *behold* (for vision, from *hold*, in the manipulation domain),
perceive (from Latin *-cipio*, "seize"), *idea* (from Greek *idein*, "see").

There is also the infrequent case of a unilateral change in the conception of the source domain. Suppose that our understanding of biology advances in a way that makes notions like "virus" as obsolete as phlogiston. Then the source vocabulary may be renewed without a concomitant change in the target.

The computer virus example was used here because it is recent enough that we can easily apprehend the main aspects of its conceptual and linguistic evolution. What research on metaphor has shown is that our conceptual systems are dominated by intricately linked networks of this sort. Because the links evolve over time and are entrenched to various degrees, the mappings we use routinely in everyday thinking and talking will be at varying stages of conceptual integration. Their cognitive importance is not reduced by the fact that we cease to be consciously aware of them.

2.2.3. "Catching up" and "getting ahead": Common Expressions That Depend on Complex Mappings

Here is an example of how general mappings produce surface language data, and how in turn such data can be used to discover underlying domains and correspondences. Consider the following.[22]

(1)   *I can't catch up with myself.*

The speaker who uttered (1) was saying that she had fallen behind in her schedule and could not "catch up," that is, could not get all of her planned activities done in the shorter time that she now had left. We take as given the basic spatial sense of *catch up*. The prototype would presumably include two entities moving along the same path, and a time interval during which one of them is behind the other and at the end of which they are at the same point on the path. Elaborations and extensions of such a prototype are easy to come by, as in cases involving short cuts, sailing regattas, and the like.[23] If applied to (1), this sense does not give us what we want: *I* and *myself* must both apparently refer to the speaker, who would require special powers of ubiquity in order to be able to race against herself. Not only is this a weird interpretation; it seems to have

22. Thanks to Jo Rubba for this example.
23. The moving objects are not necessarily on the same physical path, but they are on a common virtual path.

no connection to the intended understanding (having too many things to do). To see what is going on, we have to look at a larger sample of data and at some principles of cognitive construction.

First, there is the TIME/SPACE metaphoric mapping. In English and many other languages, we talk about time using a spatial vocabulary. Individuals and other objects "move" on a time axis from "time point" to "time point."[24] So we find ourselves *close* to Christmas, we *reach* the end of the week, we *go past* the deadline, we do something *on* Tuesday, or *at* three o'clock.[25]

For reasons that are presumably physical, times and events are also associated. An event is typically associated with a time point or time interval. Linguistically, this may be indicated by choosing a time word that denotes a time point or interval smaller, equal to, or larger than the time the event actually lasts: *The mechanic will fix your car at* **three o'clock**. *Joe will work on the car* **from 3 to 4**. *They'll do your tune-up* **on Friday**. Cultural rather than purely physical time scales are typically used.

Types of events (or of behavior, etc.) are commonly associated with time for social, cultural, and historical reasons: "wearing mini-skirts" in "the sixties," "jogging" in "the seventies," "using personal computers" in "the eighties." This cognitively conditioned kind of correspondence gives rise to interesting idioms with spatial vocabulary, such as *to keep up with the times, to be ahead of one's time*.

The cognitive construction behind such idioms is nontrivial. There is motion on two levels: the times move, and the individuals move; on a third level, we have the events typically associated with the times. An individual i is in correspondence with a type of event E in which he/she engages, and with a time t at which he/she lives. E in turn is linked to a time T (the typical time frame for events of type E). The default case is of course T = t; the individual engages in events typical of the time at which he/she lives. But if t and T are different, we have configurations as in Fig. 1.2.

For example, someone who is "behind her time" because she still jogs in the nineties instead of doing bungee jumping would occupy position i, as shown in Fig. 1.3.

We have three mappings, call them F, G, H: F maps individuals onto times at which they live and can be indicated by a simple possessive: *Caesar's time, my time* (as in: *In my time, young people knew how to*

---

24. Or the individual is fixed, and times move. *Christmas approaches; goes by; looms ahead.*
25. *On* and *at* are basic spatial prepositions.

Figure 1.2.

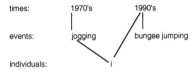

Figure 1.3.

behave). G maps types of events onto the times culturally associated with them (e.g., E onto T). H maps individuals onto types of events they engage in (i onto E). This organization automatically yields a fourth (composite) mapping, G ∘ H, linking individuals to the times typical of the events they engage, as in Figs. 1.4 and 1.5.

$$F(i) = t$$
$$G(E) = T$$
$$H(i) = E$$
$$G \circ H(i) = T$$

As an individual lives on, "her time" (this is a cognitive construct) moves along the time axis (the value assigned by F changes).[26] The value assigned by G ∘ H will also change with the individual's activities, behavior, and so on.

It is clear that if positions are measured on the time scale, and if the individual's position is assessed by means of the function G ∘ F, then, in the example considered, the individual will be at position T, when "her time" is at position *t*. She will therefore be *ahead* of "her time," if position T is ahead of position *t*, on the oriented axis.

Suppose that we hear the sentence *She is ahead of her time*. The cognitive construction outlined above will give us the abstract information that *i* (*she*) is positioned by G ∘ F at some time T, later than *t*, the time

26. Technically, what we have here is a Motion Model: In the model, the times are spatial points on an axis. The individual i is associated with two moving points occupying positions t and T on this axis. Because there is motion, the model has a time of its own having nothing to do with the axis, which is spatial in the model (even if it maps onto time in the world).

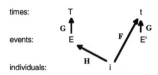

Figure 1.4.

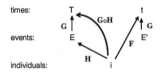

Figure 1.5.

associated with *i* by F. This yields the required real-world inference that she is engaged in activities typical of a later time than the one she is then living in. This inference is only accessible to speakers who can activate the required mappings: we must know that "she" is positioned on the time scale at T by means of G ∘ H, and that "her time" is positioned on the time scale at t by F. The English sentence *She is ahead of her time* then translates to

$$t < \text{T}$$

or, more precisely:

$$\exists \theta (t < \theta \ \& \ \text{G} \circ \text{H}(i) = \theta)$$

(there exists a time θ later than t onto which i is mapped by G ∘ H)

If we take into account the decomposition of the function G ∘ H, this formula yields:

$$\exists \theta \ \exists \varepsilon (t < \theta \ \& \ \text{G}(\varepsilon) = \theta \ \& \ \text{H}(i) = \varepsilon)$$

(there exist a time θ and an event type ε such that θ is later than t, and events ε are typical of time θ, and individual *i* engages in events of type ε at time t).

It is important to understand that the required inference is complex and cannot be made on the basis of isolated meanings of words in the English sentence: the general mappings must be accessible. Furthermore, they are productive and not limited to idioms; they account for cases like *She is already in the twenty-first century*, used to speak of someone considered extremely modern, or *They're still in the sixties*, used to speak of people who have maintained a sixties outlook and life-style. Mappings like G have pragmatically determined values upon which members of the same culture who speak the same language may of course disagree.

Given mappings of this sort, and the time-scale organization, we account for the extension of common spatiotemporal meanings of expressions like *keep up* and *catch up* to the abstract domains of fashion and life-style. The norm, as mentioned above, is for the individual i and his/her time ($t = F(i)$) to have the same position on the time scale. As both are moving in the cognitive construction, the norm (or default case) is for the individual and the time to move at the same rate. In order to *keep up* with the times, an individual i must be mapped onto $F(i)$ by the mapping $G \circ H$, that is, must be engaged in events of the type associated (by G) with $F(i)$ (the time of the present for the individual); *not to keep up* is to be mapped by $G \circ H$ onto times earlier than $F(I)$, namely, to remain engaged in activities characteristic of earlier times. An individual must *catch up* if he has *fallen behind. Catching up* entails a repositioning on the spatial scale to the expected position (the norm). In the cognitive construction under study this repositioning depends on the value of the mapping $G \circ H$. The correct inference is that the individual modifies his activities, so that $H(i) = E$, and $G(E) = F(i)$.

Let us return to the example of "catching up with oneself." The context here is one of scheduling. Events on the event scale are activities to be performed at given times by the individual. The individual is associated with the events in two different ways. At any given time, the individual is linked to the event she is actually engaged in and to the event she should be engaged in, according to the schedule. Cognitively, this abstract situation is mapped onto a concrete spatial motion model. In the model, events are positions on one path, times are positions on another. The individual is moving on two correlated paths: the path of scheduled events and the path of real times. This model is reflected by spatial vocabulary in language expressions like: *The queen went through all the events on her schedule and was exhausted when she reached the end of the day* (see Fig. 1.6).

Speed on the time scale cannot be controlled by the individual, but speed on the event scale can. The norm is for E and E′ to coincide, that is, for the individual to be moving in correlated positions on the two scales. The controllable motion on the event scale will use the uncontrollable positions correlated with the time scale as a landmark. In other words, the individual's actual position E′ will be evaluated relative to the scheduled position E, as being *behind*, or *ahead*. Because of the event/time

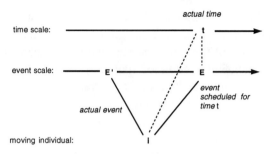

Figure 1.6.

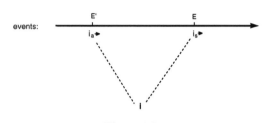

Figure 1.7.

correlations, the motion model is equivalent to one in which the individual is associated with two moving points on the *event* scale, i_s and i_a. At time t, i_s is positioned at the position of the event scheduled for t, while i_a has reached the position of the actual event engaged in at t (see Fig. 1.7).

It follows that an individual will *catch up with herself* if i_a catches up with i_s. This yields the required inference that the rate of events on the schedule speeds up (they take place faster than the norm), and eventually i finds herself engaged at time t in the event scheduled for that time.

The link between such constructions and the real world is not easy to put into words, because any talk about such situations must itself rely on the very constructions being studied. In our example, the real world is assumed to include a changing time and sequences of events. The cognitive construction includes two fixed scales, of events and times, which are *spatial*. It also includes a changing time of its own for the abstract objects in motion. In the model, spatial points on the time axis represent real time. The individual under consideration is represented by i in the model. It is mapped onto successive points t of the spatial time scale, and for each t, onto points E and E′ of the event scale. This in turn is reflected by the double motion of i_s and i_a on the event scale, and of t and T on the spatial time scale. The first position is conditioned in principle by real-world time and activities scheduled for that time; the second one by real-world activities that the individual is engaged in at that time.

This scheme allows motion in the cognitive domain to be used to draw real-world inferences: as noted above, expressions like *catch up, fall behind, and be ahead* will specify the cognitive construction in various ways by positioning the individual on the time and event scales. The configuration will then be transferable to its real-world counterparts by the kind of correspondences outlined above: if i_a is at point E', the individual is engaged in event E'; if i_s is at E, then the individual should be engaged in E.

What is remarkable in the example *I can't catch up with myself* is the reflexive pronoun *myself*. Reflexives often indicate simple coreference: in *I hate myself*, *I* and *myself* are taken to "refer" to the same person. But, more generally, as shown in *Mental Spaces* (Fauconnier 1994), we can get a reflexive if two elements of a cognitive construction are linked to the same trigger. So, in *Norman likes to read himself*, *Norman* identifies a writer a, *himself* identifies books b; b is connected to a by the pragmatic function W, linking authors and their work: $W(a) = b$. The author a in this case is the trigger, linked to b by the pragmatic function W.

The example studied here (*I can't catch up with myself*) is analogous: the motion signaled by the verb *catch up* is taking place on the spatial time scale; the two moving points are i_s and i_a, and they are linked to the same trigger i. The two points can therefore be identified by a word pointing to their common trigger, in this case *I* and its reflexive form *myself*.

The abstract nature of this entire process should not be underestimated. Converting the cultural notion of a schedule with activities to be done at certain times into a motion schema with imaginary scales is really a spectacular cognitive construction. It allows entrenched inference patterns from physical motion models to be used in reasoning about a cultural model that is objectively quite different in nature. Mappings, as we saw, play a central role. What must be underscored is that the mappings are not indicated explicitly by the language vocabulary in *I can't catch up with myself*. What the language does show is that a motion model is involved, and that the individual (here the speaker of the sentence) is a trigger for the two moving points in the model.

The account just given captures some of the complexities of this cognitive construction. Yet it is probably still oversimplified. Fauconnier and Turner (1994) argue that blending is also at work here (see Chapter 6, section 7).

It should also be noted that one cannot infer a complex model like the above on the basis of a single example or even a small range of language data. General, well-attested, mappings such as TIME/SPACE are invoked along with independently motivated principles, such as reflexive morphology for common triggers and data of different kinds (*like keep up with the times, be ahead of one's time, fall behind, move into the twenty-first century, etc.,* in our example).

Another difficulty in dealing with such phenomena is that intuitively they sometimes seem very obvious: of course we use *catch up*; how else would we talk about "catching up" on our schedule? This *illusion of simplicity* is a well-known consequence of our double status as observers and competent performers. The performer has such mastery and expertise in the manipulation of cognitive constructions that (s)he actually conceptualizes situations to some extent in terms of these very constructions, and therefore finds nothing intuitively mysterious about the corresponding data. The observer will slowly come to realize that much deeper things are going on, but will often still struggle to dissociate him/herself from her/his alter ego, the expert performer.

The illusion of simplicity is largely a consequence of our double status as observers and performers. It is hard to be the zoologist and the elephant at the same time. Perhaps this illusion is especially strong in the case of phenomena pertaining to meaning. But of course it pervades the social sciences.[27] The illusion of simplicity is strengthened by our cultural folk models about language and meaning. These models are essential to our everyday conception of talking and thinking; because we are all virtuosos in manipulating exceedingly complex mental constructions, it is important that when performing, we think of them as straightforward and direct. Tennis champions would be ill-advised to reflect while they are playing on the psychological and biological subtleties of their efforts; but their coaches and physicians are forced to take a different point of view.

Another illusion can deceive us—the *illusion of rarity*. When some example is discussed, such as the one above, *I can't catch up with myself*, even if we acknowledge its hidden complexity, we tend to see it as

---

27. There is a wealth of admirable work in sociology and anthropology that reveals the far-reaching complexities behind our apparently nonproblematic everyday life. Erving Goffman (e.g., 1959, 1974) had a special talent for bringing out this fascinating dimension. In linguistics, it was not until the advent of powerful transformational and generative techniques that the awesome formal complexity of grammatical structure was acknowledged.

a curiosity that requires a "special" explanation against a background of otherwise "well-behaved" phenomena. There seems to be a largely unconscious effort to hold to a supposedly "classical" view, by assuming that many (very interesting) phenomena are "rare," or marginal, or peripheral. This lets in some circularity, because "marginality" is easily attributed to that which eludes classical accounts.

Our approach seeks to dispel the illusion of rarity. First there is the matter of what *data* is relevant. In the natural sciences, crucial experiments are performed by creating extraordinary circumstances. Giant accelerators are built to create and observe "rare" phenomena. Or, for that matter, "rare" chemical reactions (such as $H_2 + 1/2O_2 = H_2O$) are produced in artificial laboratory environments. The same is true of cognitive language data. Statistically infrequent examples produced in statistically infrequent circumstances are apt to shed light on the basic mechanisms of everyday thinking and talking. Then there is the related question of *typicality*. There has been a tendency in modern semantics to give accounts of so-called fragments of language. The rationale was that a successful theory for a fragment could later be extended to other chunks of the language. In the same way, and for the same reason, only supposedly "simple" or "typical" conditions of use were considered; again, the hope was that more "unusual" uses would follow by extension or from as yet poorly understood pragmatic principles. This hope has not been fulfilled: fragment theories do not have natural extensions, and there are deep and interesting reasons for why this is so. To see the fallacy that we are dealing with here, suppose mathematicians attempted to extract the general properties of functions from the study of a few simple, "typical" ones, for example, $f(x) = a, f(x) = 1/x, f(x) = e^x$. Clearly, regardless of how interesting those particular functions might be, no general theory would emerge, no natural extension would apply.[28] A comprehensive theory will work in the other direction: It will seek to provide a general theory of functions that will correctly predict what happens when special conditions are imposed (so that special functions are singled out). The very same is true of meaning phenomena: The special, or "typical," cases should follow from generally applicable principles.

---

28. Studying particular functions might, however, be heuristically very useful in order to devise a general approach.

Chapter 2
Mental-Space Connections

1. The Cognitive Construction Perspective

Language, as we know it, is a superficial manifestation of hidden, highly abstract, cognitive constructions. Essential to such constructions is the operation of structure projection between domains. And therefore, essential to the understanding of cognitive construction is the characterization of the domains over which projection takes place. Mental spaces are the domains that discourse builds up to provide a cognitive substrate for reasoning and for interfacing with the world. This chapter will recapitulate the main properties of mental-space connections.

Under a standard and popular view of language organization, the joint production of form and meaning results from the divided labor of several theoretical components. The semantic component "interprets" syntactically generated structures, by assigning them context-independent truth conditions.[1] A pragmatic component, itself possibly divided into

---

1. This view of meaning is closely tied to the successful models developed for mathematical logic in the twentieth century. Tarski's foundational work in truth theory (Tarski 1956) is a common inspiration for the approach. Lewis (1972) gives an excellent description of the goals and assumptions of a truth-conditional theory of meaning. Montague (1973) has perhaps done more than anyone to carry it out, by spelling out the details of a syntax and intensional logic that might fit natural languages. An interesting aspect of Montague's theory is its full compositionality. Not only sentences, but also smaller grammatical phrases, receive logical forms and semantic interpretations. As phrases combine syntactically into larger ones, their logical forms also combine. Syntactic combination develops in parallel with semantic composition. It should be noted that Tarski's work was not aimed at natural language. In fact, one of the motivations for developing formal and truth-conditional methods, starting with Bertrand Russell, was the feeling that natural language operated unreliably, with blurs and ambiguities, and no systematic link of grammar to meaning. Formal languages would be constrained, precise, and systematic, and would provide a suitable foundation for science in general. Model-theoretic methods have been successful in logic. Although Montague and others certainly showed that they could be explored further for natural language, their ultimate failure in that domain comes as no surprise, given the considerations that motivated them in the first place.

subcomponents, is able to fix up this "literal" interpretation in various ways and to take the context into account.[2]

Although this perspective turns out to be inadequate, it has proven quite useful for the purpose of framing important questions in a precise way, and it has provided initial, powerful methods for classifying "facts" pertaining to meaning and dealing with them analytically. Until the mid-sixties, it was still assumed within linguistics that no operational study of natural language meaning was feasible unless it stemmed from a study of form.[3] The great success of research in syntax at the time suggested that the underlying levels of sentence structure discovered on the basis of distributional regularities would be the key to a genuine scientific approach to natural language semantics.[4] Then, within linguistics, semantics and pragmatics slowly emerged, with a lot of help from work that had been going on for many years in philosophy of language. It became possible to go well beyond the syntax-centered approach, and a host of semantic and pragmatic phenomena came to be studied for their own sake and in their own terms, on a par with other kinds of language data. It is noteworthy that the division into components applied not only to the theory, but to the pretheoretical data as well, so that there was often agreement as to the taxonomy of the observations—for example, "semantic scope ambiguity," "pragmatic implicature," "figure of speech," and so on.

The divided components theory, in which semantics had to do with the structure of language while pragmatics was linked to communication, filled a void. But it ran into countless difficulties. In particular, it failed to give interesting (or, for that matter, accurate) accounts of many truth-related phenomena, it tried unsuccessfully to reduce pragmatics to communication, and it did not achieve desirable generalizations and unifying explanatory principles. A number of natural-language investigators turned to a more dynamic, integrated, cognitive, outlook.

Here are some characteristics of the cognitive approach:

1. Linguistic forms are (partial and underdetermined) instructions for constructing *interconnected domains* with internal structure.

2. A strong incentive for this approach to pragmatics coupled with truth-conditional semantics was the work of Paul Grice (1967, 1975). Grice showed that, in simple cases, standard logic could be retained as a basis for literal meaning, by allowing implicatures to be added pragmatically, on the basis of conversational maxims and other pragmatic principles.

3. The impoverished view of meaning that went along with generative syntax is expounded in books of that period such as Fodor and Katz (1964) and Chomsky (1965).

4. Early generative semantics pursued this tack systematically and developed arguments for sophisticated and abstract underlying syntactic structures that looked more and more like logical forms assembled out of primitive elements.

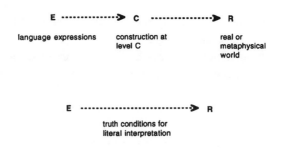

Figure 2.1.

2. This construction takes place at a "cognitive" level, call it *level C;* this level is distinct from the language structure (i.e., it is not an "underlying form," it is not a "representation" of language or of language meaning, it is not bijectively associated with any particular set of linguistic expressions).

3. Constructions at level C are not representations of the world, or representations of models of the world, or representations of models of metaphysical universes (e.g., possible worlds).[5]

4. Level C constructions, however, relate language to the real world: This is because, although they are not inherently truth-conditional, such constructions provide various real-world inferences and action patterns.

5. The cognitive view in question is realist: standard scientific methods (empirical data + explanatory hypotheses) are used to show that language use and interpretation are organized according to the first, and not the second, of the above two schemata given in Fig. 2.1.

6. The constructions at level C are different (and novel) for each case of language use; mental spaces and connections are built up as discourse unfolds; they are a function of the language expressions that come in, the state of the cognitive construction when the language expression arises, and the context of the discourse; this includes social framing, pragmatic conditions such as relevance, and real-world events perceived by the participants.

7. The primary goal of (and primary evidence for) the approach in terms of interconnected domains is *scientific generalization.*

This last point rests on standard scientific practice, namely, that wide applicability and independent motivation are a good measure for the success and validity of theoretical principles. Scientific progress is linked in important respects to the fact that such considerations (generalization,

5. See Bloom 1974, pp. 300 ff.

unification) outweigh any a priori conceptions of the studied phenomena. Moreover, they apply not only to the principles but also to the primitives within a theoretical framework.

In the current work on connected domains, scientific generalization is a guiding force at many levels and supersedes, as it should, philosophical or ontological prejudice.

Two general features are important in this regard: (a) In some respects, language treats in the same way domains whose objective counterparts (if and when they exist) are quite different. For example, it turns out that domains of the same type (mental spaces) are set up for *temporals, beliefs* (and other propositional attitudes), *images, hypotheticals, counterfactuals, dramatic situations* (plays, movies, and the like), *scenarios, quantification schemata,* and many others. (b) We find the same principles applying in areas traditionally assigned to different components. This is the case for *optimization,* for the *access principle,* and for *matching,* which play a crucial role in explaining metaphor and metonymy, pragmatic functions, referential opacity, temporal ambiguities, presupposition projection, or counterfactual grammar and interpretation. Metaphor and metonymy are traditionally assigned to rhetoric, pragmatic functions to pragmatics, opacity and ambiguity to semantics or syntax, presupposition projection to semantics and/or pragmatics. And yet, fundamental principles of level C are at work in all of these phenomena.

8. Finally, the approach recognizes the importance of connections and mappings, stressed in the previous chapter. Much of this book is devoted to exploring aspects of structure projection between mental spaces. But considerably more work lies ahead. In spite of some success in uncovering principles at work, mental space connections remain mysterious in many respects. They are, for the time being, beyond the scope of either symbolic or connectionist computational techniques, a point that raises challenging questions for cognitive science in general.

2. Space Building

2.1. Discourse Configurations

A language expression *E* does not have a meaning in itself; rather, it has a *meaning potential,*[6] and it is only within a complete discourse and in context that meaning will actually be produced. The unfolding of

6. Fauconnier 1992.

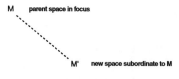

Figure 2.2.

discourse brings into play complex cognitive constructions. They include the setting up of internally structured domains linked to each other by connectors; this is effected on the basis of linguistic, contextual, and situational clues. Grammatical clues, although crucial to the building process, are in themselves insufficient to determine it.

An expression can be said to *generate* meaning: When the grammatical information it contains is applied to an existing cognitive configuration, several new configurations will be possible in principle (i.e., compatible with the grammatical clues). One of them will be produced, yielding a new step in the construction underlying the discourse.

When approached in this way, the unfolding of discourse is a succession of cognitive configurations: Each gives rise to the next, under pressure from context and grammar. A language expression entering the discourse at stage n constrains the construction of a new configuration, together with the previous configuration of stage $n - 1$ and various pragmatic factors.

The configurations produced will undergo further pragmatic elaboration.[7] They have the important characteristic of *partitioning* information, by relativizing it to different domains. The importance of partitioning for reasoning, and more general cognitive purposes, is stressed in Dinsmore (1991). The domains constructed in this fashion are partially ordered by a subordination relation: a new space M' is always set up relative to an existing space M that is in focus. M is called the parent space of M', and in subsequent diagrams the subordination relation will be represented by a dashed line as in Fig. 2.2.

The spaces set up by a discourse in this way are organized into a partially ordered lattice (Fig. 2.3). At any given stage of the discourse, one of the spaces is a *base* for the system, and one of the spaces (possibly the same one) is in *focus*. Construction at the next stage will be relative either to the Base Space or to the Focus Space.[8] Metaphorically speaking, the discourse participants move through the space lattice; their viewpoint

7. As in the example of the stern and lenient fathers discussed in Chapter 1 (section 2.2.1).
8. This is the scheme developed in Dinsmore 1991.

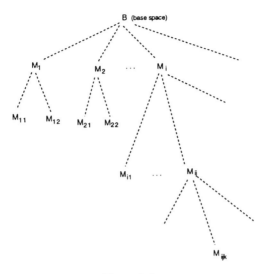

Figure 2.3.

and their focus shift as they go from one space to the next. But, at any point, the Base Space remains accessible as a possible starting point for another construction.

The mental spaces set up in this manner are internally structured by *frames* and *cognitive models,* and externally linked by *connectors,* that relate elements across spaces, and more generally, structures across spaces.

New elements can be added to spaces by linguistic expressions (e.g., indefinites) or by nonlinguistic pragmatic conditions (e.g., objects which are salient in the interaction that produces the discourse).

A sentence that appears at some stage of the discourse construction will contain several kinds of information, indicated by various grammatical devices:

- information regarding what new spaces are being set up, typically expressed by means of *space builders* (cf. below);
- clues as to what space is currently in focus, what its connection to the base is, and how *accessible* it is, this last notion to be explicated below; this information is typically expressed by means of grammatical tenses and moods;
- descriptions that introduce new elements (and possibly their counterparts) into spaces;
- descriptions or anaphors or names that identify existing elements (and possibly their counterparts);

- lexical information that connects the mental-space elements to frames and cognitive models from background knowledge (see Chapter 1); this information structures the spaces internally by taking advantage of available prestructured background schemas; such prestructured schemas can, however, be altered or elaborated within the constructions under way;
- presuppositional markings that allow some of the structure to be instantly propagated through the space configuration;
- pragmatic and rhetoric information, conveyed by words like *even, but, already,* which typically signal implicit scales for reasoning and argumentation.

A natural-language sentence is cognitively complex, because it incorporates information and building instructions at all these different levels. What kind of meaning will actually be produced depends on the mental-space configuration (generated by earlier discourse) to which the sentence actually applies.

It is essential to remember that a natural-language sentence is a completely different kind of thing from a "sentence" in a logical calculus. The natural-language sentence is a set of (underspecified) instructions for cognitive construction at many different levels.

2.2. Some Grammatical Devices for Cognitive Construction

Language has many devices to guide the construction and connection of mental spaces. Here are some of them.

Space builders. A space builder is a grammatical expression that either opens a new space or shifts focus to an existing space. Space builders take on a variety of grammatical forms, such as prepositional phrases, adverbials, subject-verb complexes, conjunctions + clause; for example, *in 1929, in that story, actually, in reality, in Susan's opinion, Susan believes..., Max hopes..., If it rains....* Grammatical techniques and strategies for building spaces in Japanese and English are compared in Fujii (1992). The psychological effects of using explicit space builders in discourse are examined by Traxler et al. (1995).

Names and **descriptions** (grammatically noun phrases). Names (*Max, Napoleon, Nabisco*) and descriptions (*the mailman, a vicious snake, some boys who were tired*) either set up new elements or point to existing elements in the discourse construction. They also associate such elements with properties (e.g., "having the name Napoleon," "being a boy," "being tired").

Tenses and **moods.** Tenses and moods play an important role in determining what kind of space is in focus, its connection to the base space, its accessibility, and the location of counterparts used for identification.

Presuppositional constructions. Some grammatical constructions, for example, definite descriptions, aspectuals, clefts, and pseudo-clefts, signal that an assignment of structure within a space is introduced in the presuppositional mode; this mode allows the structure to be propagated into neighboring spaces for the counterparts of the relevant elements.

Trans-spatial operators. The copula (*be* in English) and other "copulative" verbs, such as *become, remain,* may stand for connectors between spaces. (The general function of *be* is to stand for domain mappings; connection between spaces is a special case of this general function.) Consider a grammatical structure of the form NP_1 *be* NP_2, where NP_1 and NP_2 are noun phrases, and identify elements a_1 and a_2, respectively, such that a_1 is in space X and a_2 is in space Y. Suppose F is the only connector linking spaces X and Y. Then the language expression NP_1 *be* NP_2 will stipulate that a_2 in Y is the counterpart of a_1 in X via connector F:

$$a_2 = F(a_1)$$

Identification of elements. A crucial property of language, cognitive constructions, and conceptual links is the *Access Principle* (also called Identification principle).[9] This principle states that an expression that names or describes an element in one mental space can be used to *access* a counterpart of that element in another mental space.

Access Principle

If two elements a and b are linked by a connector F (b = F(a)), then element b can be identified by naming, describing, or pointing to its counterpart a.

---

9. The wide range of application of this principle to different kinds of domains and different kinds of connectors is studied in my *Mental Spaces* (1994). The Access Principle shows up in a variety of phenomena, and in different modalities. Van Hoek (1996) and Liddell (1995b) have shown how the signing modality for sign language exploits the Access Principle in very interesting ways. Encrevé (1988), Lakoff (1996), and Rubba (1996), among others, show unusual and powerful examples of access in psychological and cultural cases. Fauconnier and Sweetser (1996) review the typical cases.

When this indirect identification procedure is used, we say that the element named or described, a, is the *trigger,* and that the element identified, b, is the *target.*

2.3. Examples

The following examples will help give an idea of how mental-space configurations are built up. The account is somewhat simplified, in order to provide a first pass through the system.

2.3.1. Romeo and Juliet

Notation: As mentioned above, some of the lexical information in a sentence will connect mental-space elements to frames and cognitive models from background knowledge, and this will structure the space internally. Suppose, for instance, that we are engaged in a conversation about Romeo and Juliet, and the following statement is made:

Maybe Romeo is in love with Juliet.

The English sentence brings in a frame from our prestructured background cultural knowledge, "x in love with y," with two roles highlighted (the lover, x, and the loved one, y) and rich default information linked to the idealized cognitive model tied to this frame. The word *maybe* is a space builder; it sets up a *possibility* space relative to the discourse *base space* at that point. The base space contains elements a and b associated with the names *Romeo* and *Juliet,* and presumably those elements have been linked to other frames by background knowledge and previous meaning construction in the conversation. The new sentence sets up the possibility space, and creates counterparts a' and b' for a and b, which can be identified by the names *Romeo* and *Juliet,* in virtue of the Access Principle. The new space is structured internally by the frame "x in love with y," whose roles are filled by the elements a' and b'. Frames will be denoted here by capitalized words with some mnemonic value, for instance, in the present example LOVE. And the familiar notation

$$\text{LOVE } a'b' \qquad (2.1)$$

will be used to denote the internal structure added to a mental space M, namely, that elements a' and b' in space M fit the frame LOVE

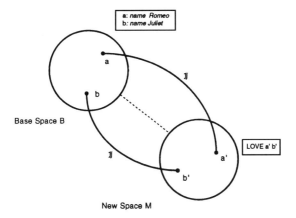

Figure 2.4.

(by filling in the grammatically specified roles of "lover" and "loved one").

In diagrammatic form, all this will be expressed in the kind of representation given in Fig. 2.4. The dashed line from B to M indicates that M is set up *relative* to B (it is subordinate to B in the lattice of discourse spaces). ℑ is the connector (in this case identity) linking a and b in space B to a′ and b′ in space M. The boxes represent internal structure of the spaces next to them.

Structure from the parent space is transferred to the new space by default. In the present case, this has the effect of associating a′ and b′ with the names *Romeo* and *Juliet,* and also with other background structure for their counterparts a and b in B. The default transfer, called *optimization,* will apply to the extent that it does not contradict explicit structure in the new space. For example, suppose that the conversation participants are talking about Romeo's *hostile* behavior toward Juliet. In B, this has the consequence that Romeo doesn't like Juliet. But this background structure will *not* transfer to the new space M, because it contradicts the *explicit* structure LOVE a′ b′. Names will not transfer either if they are explicitly ruled out in the new space, as in:

Maybe, Romeo and Juliet's names are really Dick and Jane.

This example also underscores that a′ and b′ are accessed *from the base,* by means of the names for a and b, in virtue of the Access Principle.

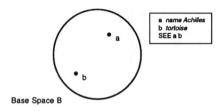

Figure 2.5.

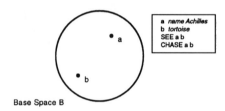

Figure 2.6.

2.3.2. Achilles and the Tortoise

Here is another example involving more spaces:

*Achilles sees a tortoise. He chases it. He thinks that the tortoise is
slow and that he will catch it. But it is fast. If the tortoise had been
slow, Achilles would have caught it. Maybe the tortoise is really a
hare.*

A cognitive construction compatible with this piece of discourse proceeds as follows:

[first sentence] *Achilles sees a tortoise.*

Achilles is a name linked to an already introduced background element
a in the Base; the indefinite noun phrase *a tortoise* sets up a new element
b. "—*sees*—" brings in the SEE frame with a and b in the roles of seer
and seen (see Fig. 2.5).

[second sentence] *He chases it.*

Background information tells us that Achilles is human and the tortoise
is an animal. This allows the anaphoric pronouns *he* and *it* to identify **a**
and **b** respectively in the Base Space. The second sentence simply adds
more internal structure to the Base (Fig. 2.6).

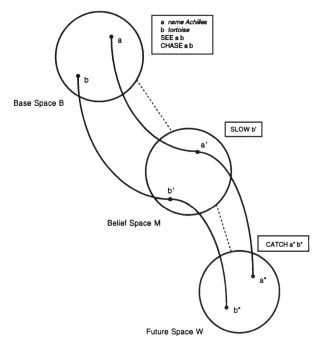

Figure 2.7.

[third sentence] *He thinks that the tortoise is slow and that he will catch it.*

The space builder *he thinks* sets up a new space M relative to B that will partition off information about Achilles' beliefs. The complement clause *the tortoise is slow and he will catch it* will structure this new space internally. Within this complement clause, we find another space builder, the future auxiliary *will;* so a third space W appears, this time relative to M. The time reference in B, has been maintained in M through the present tense; the future tense constrains event structure in W to be ordered in time after event structure in B, as shown in Fig. 2.7.

[fourth sentence] *But it is fast.*

This sentence returns us to the Base Space, which at this stage of the discourse remains the Viewpoint (more on this notion below). By default, spaces are assumed nondistinct in structure (Weak Optimization). The

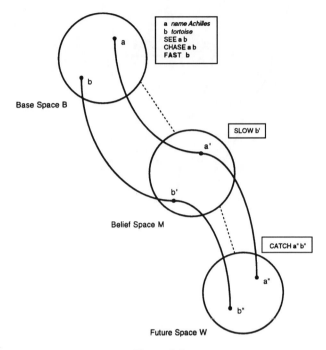

Figure 2.8.

word *but* is an explicit pragmatic signal to override this default: The structure of B differs from that of M with respect to the explicitly constructed structure [FAST b], incompatible with its counterpart [SLOW b′] (see Fig. 2.8).

[fifth sentence] *If the tortoise had been slow, Achilles would have caught it.*

The conjunction *if* sets up a hypothetical mental space H. The *distal* past perfect tense *had been* indicates that H is counterfactual (with respect to the base B). Two novel structures appear in the counterfactual space H:

SLOW b_1
CATCH $a_1 b_1$

The first (corresponding to the protasis of the conditional sentence) is a *matching condition.* It allows space H to be used for further reasoning

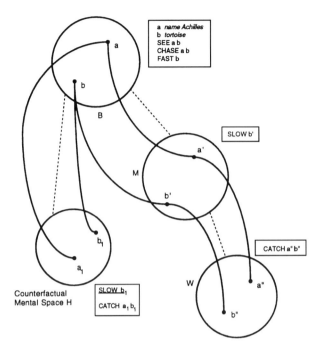

Figure 2.9.

(of the Modus Ponens variety) in later discourse: If a new space matches H with respect to this condition, it will pick up additional structure from H. The semantics of matching are studied in Chapter 5.[10] The discourse up to now is in the indicative mood. In the second part of Sentence 5, we find a new mood, the conditional *would have caught* (in the same past perfect tense as the matching condition protasis). This conditional mood is the grammatical sign that the counterfactual space is now in focus. This point will also be taken up again in more detail below. The resulting construction can be diagrammed as shown in Fig. 2.9.

[sixth sentence] *Maybe the tortoise is really a hare.*

Viewpoint is still from the Base Space. The space builder *maybe* sets up a possibility space P, in which the counterpart of the tortoise "is a" hare. The Access Principle operates here: the counterpart b_2 in the new space

10. In the more elaborate treatment of Chapter 5, space H is divided into two spaces, a Foundation and an Expansion.

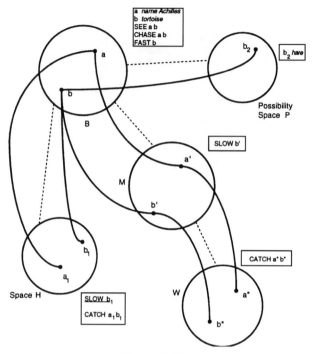

Figure 2.10.

P is accessed from the base by means of the description for its trigger b (*tortoise*). We end up with the configuration as shown in Fig. 2.10.

3. A New Look at Classic Notions

It was standard for many years within the language sciences to consider that a natural-language sentence, like a logic formula, could be assigned a context-independent truth-conditional meaning. The tradition, extending from Frege, Russell, and later Quine, to Kripke, Montague, and Lewis et al., was picked up in linguistics as well by Katz, Partee, Keenan, and many others. Many interesting problems were discussed within this framework, and such problems often find illuminating reinterpretations when examined from the domains and connections perspective. I will use the *Achilles* example to review briefly the following ones, which have received more extensive treatment elsewhere,[11] *referential opacity, scope of indefinites, presupposition projection.*

11. Fauconnier 1994, Fauconnier and Sweetser 1996.

3.1. Discourse Management: Base, Viewpoint, Focus, and Access

The key to accounting for the kind of classical problems just mentioned lies in understanding how the multiple grammatical clues in a natural-language sentence relate to the ongoing cognitive construction within a discourse.[12] As we saw in the *Achilles* example, the *sentence* is heterogeneous with respect to the mental-space construction process. It contains features responsible for a multiplicity of diverse functions:

- setting up spaces and elements, following a path within the lattice of spaces;
- structuring spaces internally;
- linking them externally by means of connectors;
- indicating what space is in focus, and what type it belongs to (moods and tenses);
- signaling what structures can be transferred by default to higher spaces (presupposition marking);
- accessing elements and their counterparts (definite descriptions, names, anaphors);
- introducing roles and linking them to values;
- establishing matching conditions for spaces that will allow deductive reasoning (e.g., *if*);
- canceling default implicatures (*but*).

In order for discourse participants to find their way through the maze of mental spaces, and to use the partitioning for drawing inferences properly, three dynamic notions are crucial: Base, Viewpoint, and Focus. At any point in the construction, one space is distinguished as Viewpoint, the space from which others are accessed and structured or set up; one space is distinguished as Focus, the space currently being structured internally—the space, so to speak, upon which attention is currently focused; and one space is distinguished as the Base—a starting point for the construction to which it is always possible to return. Base, Viewpoint, and Focus need not be distinct; more often than not, we find the same space serving as Viewpoint and Focus, or Base and Focus, or Base and Viewpoint, or all three: Base, Viewpoint, and Focus.[13]

---

12. Discourse management of mental spaces is a notion developed by Y. Takubo and discussed in Takubo 1993, Kinsui and Takubo 1990. The constructive view of logic and discourse is stressed in formally oriented work such as Dahl 1976, more than twenty years ago. Dahl and Hellman 1995 show that antecedents for anaphors are constructed dynamically in complex ways, standard coreference being just a special case.
13. Dinsmore (1991) introduces the concept of Focus space in mental-space theory. Focus and Viewpoint are studied in detail in Cutrer (1994), who adds the notion of Event space. In Chapter 3, I shall show in more detail how to find one's way through the space maze.

In the *Achilles* example, we start from a Base that is presented as corresponding to reality, or "reality" within fiction. The Base is also the Viewpoint and the Focus at the beginning of our imaginary discourse: It is, in fact, the only space configured until the appearance of the third sentence,

He thinks that the tortoise is slow and that he will catch it.

At this stage, space M is set up, and is necessarily in Focus: It is the space being structured internally; Focus has shifted from B to M. Space M is *accessed* from the Viewpoint space B. Now we come upon an underspecification in the system: space B is Viewpoint, and space M is Focus at stage 3. It is possible *in principle* for Viewpoint to remain in B at the *next* stage, or to shift to the new Focus, space M.

The next sentence in the discourse,

But it is fast.

builds structure incompatible with M, and is understood relative to B, showing that the Base B, in this case, has been *maintained* as the Viewpoint, and also that FOCUS is now shifted back to B. Notice, however, that the discourse could just as well have been continued with something like:

It probably won't take long.

which we could construe as part of Achilles' beliefs, especially if it is followed in turn by *But the tortoise is fast*. In that case, Focus has remained in M, and furthermore, Viewpoint has been *shifted* to the belief space M: The information is now presented from Achilles' point of view. *But the tortoise is fast* would return Focus and Viewpoint to the Base B.

Back to the original piece of discourse: We are back in the Base B. The next sentence,

If the tortoise had been slow, Achilles would have caught it.

sets up the counterfactual, which necessarily becomes a Focus. As before, Viewpoint is not altered; it stays in the Base, from which the next space construction (Possibility Space P) will be effected. But again the configuration at that stage is equally compatible with a Viewpoint shift. Whether or not Viewpoint has shifted is something we find out from the grammar of the next sentence. Suppose, for instance, that the next sentence had been:

He would have had a new pet.

The *grammar* of this sentence—conditional mood, past perfect tense—tells us that the counterfactual mental space H is still in Focus. And because the sentence stands alone (no space builder such as *if*), Viewpoint has also shifted: we are now presenting things from the point of view of the counterfactual situation.

3.2. Referential Opacity

The cases of referential opacity and transparency, *de re* and *de dicto* interpretations, noted by many scholars for propositional attitudes, turn out to be only special instances of the more general Access Principle. Following the work of Jackendoff (1975), and Nunberg (1978), this was in fact one of the major initial motivations for developing the theory of mental spaces.

To illustrate, consider a simple situation. Suppose James Bond, the top British spy, has just been introduced to Ursula as Earl Grey, the wealthiest tea importer, and that she finds him handsome. It is equally true that *Ursula thinks the top British spy is handsome* and that *Ursula thinks the wealthiest tea importer is handsome,* and both express the same belief. But in the first case the man introduced to Ursula has been described from the point of view of the speaker, whereas in the second he is described from Ursula's point of view. Although the first description is true and the second is false, Ursula would acquiesce to *the wealthiest tea importer is handsome,* but not (necessarily) to *the top British spy is handsome.* Descriptions and names given from the speaker's point of view are called *referentially transparent,* or *de re.* Descriptions and names given from the thinker's point of view are called *referentially opaque* or *de dicto.* Verbs like *think* or *hope* or *want* that allow such descriptions in their complements are said to create opaque contexts. Opaque contexts present a number of difficulties from a logical point of view, as noted already in medieval studies, and in modern logic by Frege, Russell, Quine, and countless others. In particular, Leibniz's Law fails in such contexts. Leibniz's Law (substitution of identicals) allows b to be substituted for a in a formula, if a = b; for example 25 can be replaced by 5^2 or by $(19 + 6)$ without changing the truth value of a mathematical statement. But in our little story, if the wealthiest tea importer is actually the very ugly Lord Lipton—that is, *the wealthiest tea importer = Lord Lipton*—then sentence (i) is true, whereas (ii) is false:

(i)   *Ursula thinks <u>the wealthiest tea importer</u> is handsome.*
(ii) *Ursula thinks <u>Lord Lipton</u> is handsome.*

Although the two names/descriptions are true of the same referent, one cannot be subsituted for the other *salva veritate*.

The complexity increases when several opaque contexts are embedded within one another:

Bill said that Iris hoped that Max wanted Ursula to think that the wealthiest tea importer was handsome.

And opacity shows up in a variety of grammatical constructions:

Ursula thinks James is smarter than he is.

In this example, the natural interpretation is referentially transparent: *than he is* yields James's actual intelligence as measured by the speaker. A referentially opaque reading has Ursula holding the contradictory belief: *James is smarter than he is.*

Discussion of opacity in the logical and philosophical tradition has tended to view it as a property of the meaning of propositional attitudes (*think, hope, want*), and of objects of belief. But in fact it follows much more generally from the Access Principle between mental spaces. According to that principle, an element in a space may be accessed by means of a description (or name) in that space or by means of a description (or name) of one of its counterparts in another space, usually a space serving as Viewpoint at that stage of the discourse construction.

So, in the case of Ursula and the spy, the following configuration (see Fig. 2.11) might have been built by discourse participants. The next step in this discourse configuration is to structure the Belief space with the additional <HANDSOME b'> corresponding to Ursula's belief that the man she has just met is handsome. Linguistically, there are two ways to do it. The element b' can be accessed directly in the Belief space now in focus. With respect to that space, the name *Grey* or the description *the wealthiest tea importer* correctly identifies b'. Sentences like the following will therefore add the proper structure:

Ursula thinks that Grey is handsome.
Ursula thinks that the wealthiest tea importer is handsome.

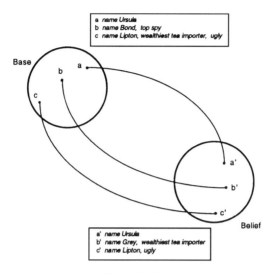

Figure 2.11.

The element b′ can also be accessed from the Base/Viewpoint space, by means of its counterpart b. With respect to that space, the name *Bond* or the description *the top spy* correctly identifies b, and can therefore be used to access b′, according to the Access Principle. Hence the following sentences also add the proper structure, using a different path through the space configuration:

Ursula thinks that Bond is handsome.
Ursula thinks that the top spy is handsome.

The first two sentences correspond, of course, to what are traditionally called opaque readings. The last two correspond to transparent ones. Their existence and properties follow directly from the Access Principle.

An essential point, often made in the mental-space literature, is that the same ambiguities show up no matter what kind of space (belief, time, movie, counterfactual) we are dealing with. It is the multiple connecting paths available in a partitioned configuration that yield multiple understandings. It is not the content of the mental spaces (propositional attitudes, time, geographical space, images).

Also, the number of paths for a given sentence is not fixed. What matters are the spaces available in a particular discourse. The more spaces accessible from the Focus, the more connecting paths there will be, and consequently, the more potential understandings for the sentence. For example, the sentence *If I were your father, I would help you* sets up a minimum of three spaces and has a minimum of three understandings, as outlined in Chapter 1, section 2.2.1. But if more spaces are available, there will be more readings. Fauconnier (1990b) shows that if the context for this sentence is the making of a movie, and the speaker is Kirk Douglas and the addressee Jane Fonda, there will be nine readings, because of the increased number of spaces and referential access paths.

A sentence in itself has no fixed number of readings. It has a potential for generating connections in mental-space configurations. The number of readings will be a product of this potential and the spaces available (and accessible) in a particular context.

The *Achilles* example provides a similar instance of the Access Principle at work. Consider the last sentence of the minidiscourse:

Maybe the tortoise is really a hare.

This is a case of referential transparency: the definite description *the tortoise* is used to refer to what in the modal context is not a tortoise but a hare. A referentially opaque interpretation is also available for this sentence taken in isolation, implying somewhat contradictorily that the same animal could be simultaneously a hare and a tortoise. The two interpretations are available in principle, because the element b_2 can be accessed either directly within the Focus space, by means of characteristics associated with b_2 in that space, or indirectly from a Viewpoint space (here the Base), by means of characteristics associated with the counterpart of b_2 in the Viewpoint space.

Consider a slightly different piece of discourse:

Achilles is chasing a hare. He believes that the hare is a tortoise. And he believes he is faster than the tortoise.

Figure 2.12 shows the corresponding mental-space configuration. This time, in the last sentence, we find the "referentially opaque" interpretation: b' is identified directly from within the space in Focus, namely Belief Space M.

In principle, at any point in the discourse a mental-space element can be accessed from the Base, or the Viewpoint, or the Focus. If one space is simultaneously Base, Viewpoint, and Focus, then of course no distinctions will appear. But as soon as Viewpoint, or Focus, or both, get shifted, then different accessing strategies will become available.

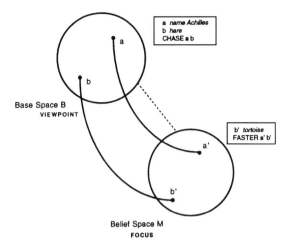

Figure 2.12.

When we look at this, not in terms of the unfolding discourse, but in terms of the isolated sentence, and its *potential* for meaning construction, it follows that a sentence containing an explicit grammatical space builder, which necessarily shifts Focus, always has the potential for *more than one* accessing strategy. The sentence *Achilles believes that he is faster than the tortoise,* because it contains the explicit space builder *Achilles believes,* will always appear in a discourse containing at least two spaces, Base and Focus, and so the definite description *the tortoise* can in principle be linked to at least two different accessing strategies: one in which it directly identifies an element in the Focus Space, as in the above minidiscourse, and one in which it identifies the counterpart of that element in the Base. This latter interpretation is called for in a reversed discourse situation from the first, such as:

Even though he thinks it's a hare, Achilles believes that he is faster than the tortoise.

Leaving aside the pragmatic scale constructed by *even,* the corresponding mental-space configuration would be as shown in Fig. 2.13. This time, the *same* sentence is used to access b′ in M through its counterpart b in the Base/Viewpoint mental space B. We have the *de re* interpretation. When a sentence is examined in isolation, and its interpretations are studied, it is necessary to construct implicitly a discourse in which to interpret it. By default, a *minimum* discourse is usually chosen, with the

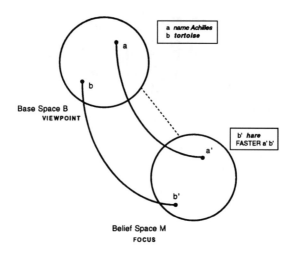

Figure 2.13.

implication that this will yield the "real," "core," context-independent meaning of the sentence. This implication is unwarranted; there is no reason why the *particular* configuration associated with a linguistic expression in a minimum discourse should contain the defining characteristics for the meaning *potential* of that expression in *other* discourses.

Consider once again our example *Achilles believes that he is faster than the tortoise.* But suppose that the situation is richer in connections and spaces than the "minimum" default discourse. Then possible interpretations for this sentence will proliferate. In fact, far from being limited to the two we have envisaged (traditional *de re* and *de dicto*), the number of *logically distinct* interpretations is theoretically unbounded.

Suppose, for example, that in the situation where the sentence is used we are talking about a play in which humans play the roles of animals. One of the actors is Achilles, who plays the role of the hare. Another actor is Paris, who plays the role of the tortoise. Achilles, however, is under the mistaken impression that another third actor, Hermes, is playing the role of the tortoise. And the conversation participant knows this. Given this scenario, when our example sentence comes along in the discourse, the cognitive configuration has already been set up as shown in Fig. 2.14.

B is the Base, with current information in the conversation about the real-life actors. P is a space subordinate to B, with current information about the play. M is set up relative to B, with information regarding the beliefs of Achilles. And Q, subordinate to M, is structured to reflect

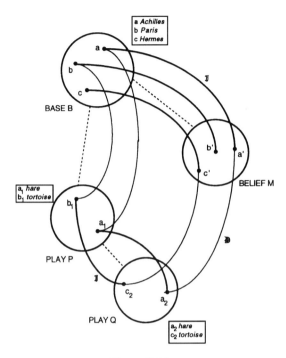

Figure 2.14.

current information about Achilles' beliefs concerning the play. Two connectors operate: Identity $\Im$, and Drama $\mathfrak{D}$, which connects actors and characters.

This richer configuration offers more ways for the Access Principle to operate. When the target sentence *Achilles believes that he is faster than the tortoise* comes into the discourse, it puts either M or its subordinate Q in Focus. This leaves several construction possibilities compatible with the incoming sentence:

(1) If Viewpoint is from the Base, and Focus on Q, *the tortoise* can identify c_2 in Q directly, while *Achilles* names a, and thus provides access to its counterpart a_2, via the connection from B to M to Q (connection $\mathfrak{D}\circ\Im$). That will yield the additional internal structure in Q:

FASTER $a_2 c_2$

This structure will reflect a belief of Achilles regarding the play: that the hare is faster than the tortoise. It may have effects on the way in which he thinks he must play his part.

(2) If Focus is on the belief space M, the description *the tortoise* for c_2 in Q can be used to *access* the counterpart of c_2 in space M, namely c', while the anaphor *he* accesses a'. The corresponding additional structure for space M will be:

FASTER $a'c'$

This reflects Achilles' belief that he is faster than Hermes. But notice the subtle shift in viewpoint: it reflects this belief of Achilles through Achilles' (mistaken) view of Hermes as the actor playing the tortoise.

(3) If the Viewpoint is now P ("the play") within the Base, and the Focus is again on M, the belief space, then b' may be accessed through its counterpart b_1, yielding the structure:

FASTER $a'b$

This time, the belief reflected is that Achilles is faster than Paris.

(4) Because comparatives can operate across mental spaces (Fauconnier 1985), the following interpretations are also available:

$4'$: FASTER a' c_2 [Achilles thinks that he (the human) is faster than the tortoise in the play.]

$4''$: FASTER a' b_1 [The speaker evaluates the speed of the tortoise to be x and the speed which Achilles believes himself to be capable of to be y, and says that y is greater than x.]

(5) Now this may seem like an already large number of interpretations; but it is only the subset of interpretations available for the sentence relative to the special space configuration corresponding to the imagined situation.

In the spirit of autonomous semantics and logic, consider the wider question: What are the constructions compatible with our sentence, within a *four-space configuration with two connectors?* The answer: many. The definite description *the tortoise* could describe elements in M and/or B, and it could have counterparts in P and Q, via either connector $\mathfrak{F}$ or connector $\mathfrak{D}$. I will not attempt to go through the tedious list of combinations, which involve a tortoise in the real world, beliefs of Achilles as to who that tortoise is, fictional representations of the (real) tortoise in the play, viewed either from Achilles' point of view or from the speaker's, the real tortoise playing the role of other animals in the play, and so on.

The bottom line is this: because of the many spaces a description may originate in, because of the many ways in which counterparts may be accessed, a given sentence does not have a fixed set of readings; rather, it has a *generative potential* for producing a set of interpretations with respect to any discourse mental-space configuration. The referential opacity/transparency distinction noted by scholars is but one very special and very simple case of this potential: the case in which the number of spaces is limited to two, and in which the sentence contains an explicit space builder for one of the two spaces. When the notions of role and value are brought in, the number of configurational possibilities increases even further (cf. Fauconnier 1985, 1986; Sweetser 1990b; Sakahara 1996).

3.3. Scope of Indefinites

In the same way that sentences are grammatically underspecified as to the origin of definite descriptions (the mental space of the named or described element), they are also typically underspecified as to where an indefinite description introduces a new element. So if the kind of situation imagined above gives rise to the sentence

Achilles believes he will catch a rabbit

the *grammar* tells us that a new element d fitting the frame Rabbit is set up, but it does not specify in what mental space.

Here are some interpretations corresponding to different choices for insertion points:

- Insertion directly into W, the future mental space set up (by *will*) relative to M: d has no counterparts in any of the other spaces. The rabbit is completely nonspecific: We are not talking about any particular rabbit, either in reality or in the play, nor does Achilles have any particular rabbit in mind; there are still two subinterpretations, however, depending on whether the insertion is in W only, or in the subspace Q′ of W associated with future events in the play.
- Insertion of d into the Base, with a counterpart d′ in W; this is one of the "specific" readings, where the speaker commits herself to the existence of the rabbit, about which Achilles has certain beliefs (including, perhaps, that it is a hare, or a tortoise, or . . .).
- Insertion of d into P (the "play" relative to the base); the relevant counterpart of d is in Q′ (Achilles' beliefs about future events in the play): The play, as understood by the speaker, has a character which is a rabbit, and we are talking about Achilles' beliefs regarding future events in the play involving that character and the one played by Achilles. Achilles does not have to believe that this rabbit is a rabbit (i.e., the counterpart of d in Q can fit into frames different from the ones for d in P).

- Insertion of d into M (Achilles' belief space), with a target counterpart d' in the future-belief space W: Achilles, this time, does have a rabbit in mind, and has future beliefs about it.
- Insertion of d into Q (Achilles' view of the play), with a counterpart in Q' (Achilles' beliefs about future events in the play): Achilles, this time, does believe that one of the characters in the play is a rabbit (and he could be mistaken, from the speaker's standpoint), and the sentence is about beliefs that Achilles holds concerning his own character (the hare) and the rabbit character.

There is nothing vague about the number of such interpretations: It is a function of the number of spaces already set up, and their accessibility relations. The crucial point, which has been stressed over and over again in mental-space research, is that underspecification combined with the Access Principle yields all the traditional scope distinctions in simple cases, and yields *far more* in the general case. Contrary to traditional scope analyses, the number of interpretations exceeds (in principle) by more than one the number of operators explicitly mentioned in the sentence (in our example, *believes* and *will*).

3.4. Presupposition Projection

Natural languages have grammatical devices for marking some of the internal structure of mental spaces as *presupposed*. This is a powerful expressive feature because it allows structure to be propagated by default through the lattice of mental spaces built up as part of an ongoing discourse. As a result, large amounts of structure are added, with a minimum of explicit lexical information. Grammatical presuppositional constructions include definite descriptions, factives, clefts and pseudo-clefts, aspectual verbs and adverbs, and iteratives.

The king of France is (not) bald presupposes that there *is* a king of France (definite description). *Hilda knows (doesn't know) that her son is a thief* presupposes that Hilda's son is a thief (factive). *It was (not) Romeo that Juliet loved* presupposes that Juliet loved someone (cleft construction). *Luke stopped (didn't stop) smoking* presupposes that Luke smoked. *Chicago defeated Oakland too* presupposes that another team defeated Oakland, or that Chicago defeated another team than Oakland (iterative).

Over the years, the problem of presupposition projection has received extensive attention and given rise to extremely interesting work. In traditional terms, the *projection problem* is about sentences: When do presuppositions of embedded clauses give rise to presuppositions of the entire sentence? Work in Schiebe (1975), Dinsmore (1981, 1991), Fauconnier (1985/1994) shows that we are dealing with a discourse phenomenon, and that a more satisfactory way of posing the problem is to ask how information grammatically introduced as presupposed relative to one mental space can be either propagated to other spaces or blocked from being propagated.

We can improve on previous formulations of Presupposition Float by invoking the following general principle:

Presupposition Float

A presupposed structure Π in mental space M will propagate to the next higher space N, unless structure already in M or N is incompatible with Π, or entails Π.

Informally: *A presupposition floats up until it meets itself or its opposite.*

To say that a structure "propagates" from space X to another space Y is to say that, if it is satisfied for elements x, y, . . . in X, it is satisfied for their counterparts x′, y′, . . . in Y, via some connector $\mathfrak{C}$. As usual, we find structure mappings involved in matching processes that transfer structure.

So consider, for example, a familiar case like:

Sue believes Luke has a child, and that Luke's child will visit her.

The space building proceeds roughly as follows:

Base B: elements a (*name Sue*), b (*name Luke*)

Belief Space M, introduced relative to B: new element c, counterpart b′ for b, via the Identity connector $\mathfrak{I}$, new structure CHILD c b′.

Future Space W, introduced relative to M: counterparts a″, b″, c″, for a, b, c; new structure VISIT c″ a″; presupposed structure <b″ *HAS CHILD*>. This structure is grammatically marked as presupposed through the use of the definite description construction (definite article *the*).

The Presupposition Float Principle prevents this presupposed structure from floating up from W into M, because explicit structure in M (CHILD c b′) already entails <*HAS CHILD*> for the counterparts c and b′ in

M of c′ and b″ in W. Because the presupposition does not float up to M, it cannot, a fortiori, float up to the Base: it has been halted at the W level. This ensures that the piece of discourse does not globally presuppose (or entail) that Luke has children.

Notice that although the presupposition does not float all the way up, it is not canceled: It remains in force at the W level. This is important in principle: A presupposition will float up into higher spaces, until it is halted. It will then *remain* in force for the mental spaces into which it has floated. In other words, inheritance is not an "all or nothing" process. The general issue is: *What spaces inherit the presupposition?* The vast literature on presupposition projection typically limits itself to asking if the "whole sentence" inherits the presupposition. In our terms, this amounts to asking if the Base Space of a minimum discourse configuration inherits the presupposition, in other words, if the presupposition floats *all the way up*. To account for the full range of semantic entailments, this is insufficient; the more general question has to be answered: *How far up does the presupposition float?* The answer to the general question, given by the Presupposition Float Principle, will of course subsume the answer to the special question: Does it float to the Base?

Now, consider a related example:

Jane hopes that Sue believes that Luke's children will visit her.

An additional space H (set up by *Jane hopes*, relative to B) serves to launch M. The presupposition <*HAS CHILDREN*>, satisfied for b″ in M, will float up freely into H and then into B. This amounts, for the speaker, to assuming that Luke has children, and that Jane and Sue assume that Luke has children.

But it is essential to note that even though this type of *Spreading* is warranted by the minimal discourse that could be associated with this sentence, it could be *canceled* by either prior or later discourse. Our example sentence could occur in a discourse where it is already assumed that Luke has no children or that Jane thinks he doesn't. Then the presupposition would be halted at the B level, or at the H level, by incompatible preexisting structure. In other words, the default case here is for the presupposition to spread all the way up, but the sentence is perfectly compatible with a discourse preventing or canceling some of that spreading. This may happen under pressure from *later* discourse, when we are told that "in fact" Luke has no children. The construction will be maintained, *except* for the floating into B, which is now superseded by stronger explicit information.

In terms of processing meaning construction, this observation raises some key issues: It means that some aspects of the constructed space configurations are more stable than others. Specifically, the structures that have been obtained *implicitly* (e.g., through Presupposition Float) must be stored as cancelable, at least in the short term.

Finally, notice the possible interplay of Float with *Access*. It was assumed, in discussing the previous example, that the expression *Luke's children* had introduced structure directly into the bottom space M. But, as we saw in section 2.3.2, it could equally well describe an element in a higher space, B or H, which would then serve to access a counterpart in M. This yields possible interpretations for the sentence, in which the speaker and Jane, but not Sue, assume that Luke has children, or in which the speaker only, but neither Jane nor Sue, is assumed to assume that Luke has children.

As noted in Fauconnier (1985/1994) and Kay (1992), other types of presupposition can be used in this way to provide access from the top rather than floating from the bottom. Very generally, the underlying forces in the discourse construction have the aim of spreading structure across spaces, using minimal linguistic effort, through powerful default procedures. We find that Spreading happens in both directions: top to bottom (through Access), and bottom to top (through Floating).

The Presupposition Float Principle handles in a very general way examples that have proved troublesome in presuppositional analysis. For example:

If John has children, then John's children are bald.

The *if . . . then* construction sets up a hypothetical (foundation) space H relative to the base B, and an expansion space E relative to H (see Chapter 5 for details). In H, the information that John has children is set up nonpresuppositionally (*John has children*). In E, it is set up presuppositionally (*John's children*). The presupposition floats from E up to H and "meets itself" in space H. It cannot float up any higher. It follows that it will not be propagated to the Base. This correctly reflects that the sentence as a whole does not presuppose that John has children, as opposed to—say—*If John is here, then John's children are in New York.*

Another familiar example discussed by Soames (1982) is:

If Oakland beats Montreal, Chicago will beat Montreal too.

The iterative *too* brings in the presupposition Π in E that a team other than Chicago has beaten Montreal. Π is entailed by the nonpresuppositional structure in H corresponding to *Oakland beats Montreal,* and therefore does not float up to H. The sentence indeed does not presuppose that any other team has yet beaten Montreal.

It should also be noted that space partitioning does not reflect "the world," but rather discourse information about the world at various stages. Spaces will reflect what is known or not known. For example, a form *Either A or B* will set up two spaces relative to the Base, which must both be *compatible* with the Base (i.e., with current knowledge at that stage of the discourse). This means that the new structures set up by A and B, respectively, are each compatible with the Base structure, even though they may be incompatible with each other. Consequently, if A carries a presupposition Π that is incompatible with B, that presuppositon will not float up to the Base: this is because the Base is constrained (by the semantics of *either . . . or*) to be compatible with B-structure; this makes Π incompatible with the Base and prevents it from being inherited, by virtue of the Presupposition Float Principle.

To illustrate, consider the standard example:

Either Luke just stopped smoking or he just started to smoke.

One disjunct has the presupposition that Luke was a smoker, the other that he wasn't. Incompatibility with the Base prevents such presuppositions from floating up.

As Soames (1982) has shown in detail, examples like the ones above, and many others, cannot be integrated into a coherent treatment within the sentence-based accounts typically proposed by combinatorial or cancellation approaches to the projection problem (e.g., Karttunen 1973; Karttunen and Peters 1979; Gazdar 1979).

Mental-space analysis offers a uniform, general, and broader account of presupposition phenomena. Furthermore, the account is *principled,* because it relates presupposition projection to the structure-building process of Spreading: maximizing the amount of structure introduced with respect to the linguistic means employed.

3.5. Grammar and Meaning

The examples briefly reviewed thus far show that linguistic form plays a role in meaning construction that goes far beyond the assignment of satisfaction conditions. The next chapter, dealing with tense and mood, will look at yet other intricate ways in which grammar prompts the construction of appropriate space configurations and viewpoints. The following general aspects of the meaning and form association are noteworthy.

1. A language expression can do many things at once. The *Achilles* sentences we looked at open spaces, set up new elements, structure spaces internally, and connect spaces to others in the space configuration. This is one important difference between sentences and logical formulas, which only specify satisfaction conditions within a domain. It is one reason for the difficulties encountered in trying to reduce sentences to logical forms; even though an important function of sentences is indeed to specify satisfaction conditions, it is only one of several functions, and it may target more than one space at the same time.

2. The effect of a language expression depends on the space configuration it operates on. The space-building *instructions* associated with particular grammatical constructions are unique. For example, in English:

$a N$: set up a new element that fits the frame called up by N.

$NP_1 BE NP_2$: connect the elements identified by NP_1 and NP_2, respectively.

(N is a noun, NP a noun phrase.)

But the effects of such instructions may be widely different, depending on the configuration they operate on when they come into the discourse. A new element will have three places to go to if three spaces have already been set up at the discourse stage where the indefinite description comes in; it will have only one if the Base is the only space in the configuration. *BE* will connect spaces differently depending on what connectors (space mappings) are active at the relevant discourse insertion point. There are multiple possibilities for instantiating language instructions; this important aspect of meaning construction is explored in some detail in *Mental Spaces* (Fauconnier 1994). The multiple possibilities do not stem from structural or logical ambiguities of the *language form;* they stem from its *space-building potential:* The language form contains *underspecified* instructions for space building. It can apply to infinitely many kinds of input; and for any given input there is a finite number of outputs that it can yield.

3. Language expressions underspecify cognitive constructions. This point is related to the previous one; there will typically be many configurations formally compatible with the space-building instructions carried by grammatical constructions. They will be partly resolved by pragmatic considerations involving strategies such as noncontradiction, relevance, prototypicality, default options, and so on.[14]

4. Some logical properties of sentences in isolation are really special cases of their potential for space construction. For example, the so-called *de re/de dicto* and specific/nonspecific ambiguities are a simple consequence of the general Access Principle, when restricted to the case of two spaces set up by the same sentence.

4. Truth, Reference, and Pragmatics

4.1. Ambiguity, Intensionality, and Discourse Configurations

The initial and important reason for studying space configurations was that they provide general answers to puzzles of language and meaning that are usually associated with sentence logic.

When a sentence is looked at in isolation, we come up with the typical interpretations for that sentence, and we try to match up the sentence with logical forms (or representations) that will account for the observed "meanings." But when a sentence is correctly understood to be making an overall contribution to cognitive discourse construction, we find that the same "meaning," conceived of as building instructions, can give rise to different "interpretations," depending on what existing configuration such instructions are applied to, and how they are applied; the "how" comes into play because the building instructions typically underspecify the construction: There can be more than one way to elaborate an existing configuration in conformity with the instructions carried by the linguistic form of the sentence.

There are two important consequences: (1) The logical properties of isolated sentences follow from the general principles for building configurations; and furthermore, logical properties that are not apparent in isolation but emerge in full discourse are also accounted for.

---

14. To say this, however, is not to resolve the incredibly difficult problem of how, in practice, strategies are chosen. In fact, although pragmatic factors reduce available choices considerably, participants in communication often choose different strategies, and there are far more misunderstandings than we are usually aware of. The misunderstandings get noticed only when they lead to serious clashes of relevant and clearly visible entailments.

(2) Logical forms commonly assigned to isolated sentences correspond to observations that a philosopher, a logician, a linguist, is liable to make, but they are not representations within the theory itself. They are derivable from the theory, insofar as they correspond to special cases of space configurations. The bound variables of logic and linguistic anaphors (pronouns in particular) are similar in some ways, but very different in others. The space elements, on the other hand, which are indirectly responsible for the existential quantifications, behave consistently as a basis for anaphora, regardless of what spaces they happen to be in.

This last point can be emphasized: It is a constant assumption throughout this work that grammar is cognitively motivated and, correspondingly, that understanding grammar in its context of use (rather than in purely autonomous structural terms) will yield insight into cognitive organization. Simplicity arguments follow from this general assumption: We seek links between cognitive constructs and grammatical features that are as direct and general as possible, and we see such simplicity, directness, and generality as counting heavily when evaluating any analysis.[15]

4.2. Truth and Reference

In the configurations we looked at, frame properties were assigned to elements. This is not the usual sense for the notion of property; properties like "tortoise" hold of entities in the world, not of cognitive constructs (like "element a"). But it is also noteworthy that we can understand discourses like the ones above in the absence of actual entities (real tortoises and the like) being referred to. How is this possible? How can configurations relate to the real world and to the way that we apprehend it?

Our folk theories are relevant here. When we talk, we assume that there are indeed objects and properties in the real world and that, given an object and a property, there is a fact of the matter as to whether the object has the property or not. Now, take any space in which an element a is assigned property P. Suppose we link a with real-world object A. P(a) counts as "true," under that matchup, if object A has property P,

---

15. Strangely, within linguistics and philosophy of language, this commonsensical scientific guideline is sometimes missing. Indirect or convoluted solutions have some appeal, perhaps because the search for an autonomous language faculty triggers a kind of reverse Ockham's razor effect.

and "false" otherwise. It does not matter whether we have or think we have an actual procedure for checking that properties hold of objects. All that matters is the assumption that there are objects and that, in some deep absolute sense, they have or do not have the properties we consider. It does not directly matter, either, whether or not this assumption itself is right as long as its commonsense credibility is sustained. And this credibility is certainly sustained for common objects and properties that we deal with in everyday life.

What counts here is the social consensus on objects and properties in various situations. When presented with a kettle, say, and asked about its color, we do not, outside of philosophical circles, ask whether there is really an object there that everyone is referring to, or whether it makes any sense to predicate the property "black" in such a situation. We simply concur in identifying an object and assume that it is either black or not black. Yet, as Charles Travis (1981) shows in great detail, the actual conditions under which the very same kettle might count as black or not black are a complex function of the context; realistically, there are no absolute properties. Again, this does not matter for the purpose at hand: It is sufficient to assume that if a cognitive space were matched up with real-world objects and relations, the interpretation conditions of the type Travis discusses would also be given, so that there is a fact of the matter as to whether the space fits the "real" situation.

Once we have this type of implicit assumption, spaces take on "meaning" in the realistic sense: Given a matchup of space elements with real-world objects, relation specifications within the space will be either true or not true.

Remember that all this is independent of the much harder question of how we actually connect configurations to real-world situations. A "property" that shows up in cognitive constructions is really part of an ICM ("idealized cognitive model"),[16] and such ICMs are matched to the real world in complex ways. What counts here is only the idealized assumption that, in a given situation and for a given matchup between elements and real-world objects, the space fits or does not fit the situation, in the sense that the objects have or do not have the properties assigned to the space elements associated with them. How people achieve (or try to achieve) social and psychological consensus on such matchups is another matter.

16. See Lakoff (1987).

Once this theoretical matchup possibility is granted, we can turn to a more intriguing feature of the space configurations: They can be manipulated, operated on, and so forth, in the absence of any actual particular matchup. This is why we can process and "understand" a minidiscourse like the one in section 2.3.2 in the absence of any real person called Achilles, or of any real tortoise, hare, or rabbit. We can understand the "content" of Achilles' belief even if we have no precise idea of what a tortoise looks like, simply by assuming that property F ("tortoise") is in fact one that applies or does not apply to given entities. We may have many ideas about tortoises, in the sense that we associate many other properties with property F, but it doesn't really matter that participants in a discourse like the one in 2.3.2 might have wildly different networks of properties associated with F, unless such properties happen to contribute to the explicit inference production in the discourse; then there can be arguments, misunderstandings, disagreement, and so on, among the participants.

The manipulation of space configurations in the absence of a real-world matchup would be no more than a solipsistic exercise were it not for the crucial implicit assumption that we know in principle how to match worlds with configurations. The tricky part is that this is an assumption we make when we talk and think, an assumption that is socially essential, but also one that is not factually supported by our behavior.

In the rest of this book we shall encounter many cases of space constructions that are not intended to serve in direct matchups with the real world but can nevertheless yield important real-world inferences. One of the motivations for such constructions is to link new domains with existing ones, so that some of the known logical structure of the existing domain can be exported directly into the new one. This is a powerful, nondeductive means of producing large classes of inferences that can be used in a particular context and situation. It is also a way of structuring an understanding of a particular discourse situation.

To sum up, truth and reference are far from absent in the overall theory of space configurations; because spaces contain elements with assigned properties, they have a potential for acquiring real-world truth values under specific matchups of elements with objects. And yet the configurations can be operated on to yield inferences and additional structure without instantiating any of the potential matchups.

One suspects that this feature of space construction is a major factor behind some unusual aspects of human creativity. When language is

narrowly limited to its information-carrying function, there has to be a
matchup: Giving correct information is to refer to things and beings, and
to say something true about them. But for most other uses, for instance,
scientific and literary imagination, social interaction, argumentation,
proof and persuasion, poetry, swearing, potential reference is sufficient.

4.3. Pragmatics

Mathematical formulas are designed to give structural information explicitly and unambiguously. As a result, each mathematical formula
gives comparatively little information, but does so quite thoroughly. Language expressions, in contrast, seem designed to yield huge amounts of
structure. This happens in the following way: Some words and grammatical constructions bring with them an array of background knowledge,
including frames, cognitive models, default assumptions, encyclopedic
information; pragmatic functions are signaled by words like *be;* as *be*
does not identify the particular function or mapping, it is inferred on
the basis of context plus background knowledge and models; similarly,
expressions like the one studied in Chapter 1, section 2.2.3 (*I can't catch
up with myself*) bring in complex mappings and connections for their interpretation, even though such mappings are not indicated by the words
in the sentence; when spaces are set up relative to other spaces, default
structuring processes like *optimization* operate to provide structure not
explicitly indicated; presuppositions introduced in one space float up
through adjacent spaces; extensive *projection mappings* (Chap. 1, sec.
1) are also set up, using very few words: a metaphorical connection signaled by just one of its connected pairs will project one entire domain
onto another, not just the members of the pair; finally, rich sets of implicatures come into spaces along with the frame-based relations that
are explicitly specified; constructions are often set up for the purpose of
bringing in such implicatures.

All these diverse kinds of structuring contribute to building up a space
configuration, and new sentences that come along in the discourse
typically take such prior construction into account: For example, words
like *but* cancel implicatures, pronouns may identify elements introduced
covertly into spaces by optimization, words like *therefore* signal deductive relationships that may not have been explicitly stated, and so on.

Much of this is pragmatics. Space configurations are built up seman-
tically and pragmatically at the same time. There is no configuration

corresponding only to the semantic information that would later be patched up by the pragmatics. Incidentally, this does not imply that the division between pragmatics and semantics disappears. We are free to call some of the processes involved in the construction semantic and others pragmatic; but there will not be any separate representations involved. The isolated sentences have a semantics in the sense that they provide instructions for space construction. Their actual contribution to a particular discourse will depend on the configuration that is built up for that discourse; because much of the contribution from a particular sentence will usually depend on its conjoined action with other features of the construction, there will not be, in the present approach, anything like the specific "content" of an expression separable from the rest of the construction.

Chapter 3
Tense and Mood

We have seen how human thought, as it unfolds, sets up elaborate configurations of mental spaces linked to each other and to background knowledge. Discourse management is essential (Takubo 1993; Takubo and Kinsui 1992; Kinsui and Takubo 1990). The thinker, speaker, hearer, discourse participant must keep track of the spaces set up, their content, the links between them, and the order in which they appear. The process is a dynamic one. At any stage, one must know, or be able to figure out, how to move discursively through the configuration. Specifically, this means knowing at a given stage what space is the Base, what space is currently the Viewpoint, from which others will be accessed or constructed, and what space is in Focus—where meaning is currently being constructed. Two dimensions of human thought and human experience seem especially important in this regard: *time* and *epistemic distance*. All languages devote considerable grammatical resources to these two dimensions, and they are characterized in relative rather than absolute terms. Although the cognitive systems that reflect these two dimensions are invariably complex, the guiding ideas are simple. In moving (mentally) from one mental space to another, we try to keep track of the time shifts and epistemic shifts between the spaces in focus. Relative time is simply a relation between times of events in the two spaces. Epistemic distance is the "reality" status of one space with respect to another. Take, for example, the very short story *Max is happy. He won. Otherwise he would be sad.* We move from the Base (Max happy) to a "past" space (Max win), earlier in time than the Base, and then to a counterfactual space (Max not win. Max sad), simultaneous in time with the Base, but epistemically shifted because marked as unreal (relative to the Base).

The challenge for a natural language is to provide means of keeping track of time and epistemic value through much longer stretches of thought and discourse. Tense and mood are the devices of choice for doing this generally. Recent work has uncovered elegant principles that languages use for space tracking. In this chapter, I will go over some of the main features of such cognitive systems, as developed for time and tense, first by John Dinsmore, and then by Michelle Cutrer. The sections on mood and epistemic distance draw mainly from work done by Eve Sweetser and Errapel Mejias-Bikandi.

1. Tense

1.1. Viewpoint, Focus, and Time Paths

As outlined in Chapter 2, any space configuration will include a Base, a Viewpoint, and a Focus. To these three discourse primitives, we add a fourth, Event. These primitives are assigned to the discourse spaces dynamically: As discourse and thought progress, Viewpoint, Focus, Event, and even Base can shift from one space to another or be conflated in the same space. Informally, the Base space is an anchor for the configuration, often the space we start in, and one we can easily come back to. A Viewpoint space is the one from which other spaces are currently being built or accessed. The Focus space, as explained by Dinsmore, is where content is currently being added, and the Event space (often but not always the same as the Focus) corresponds to the time of the event or state being considered.

To give an informal idea of how this works, consider once again a simple, very short piece of discourse.

Max is twenty-three. He has lived abroad. In 1990, he lived in Rome. In 1991 he would move to Venice. He would then have lived a year in Rome.

Without justification for the moment, here are the space-building dynamics associated with the production and/or understanding of this ministory.

(1) We start with a single space, which is the Base, and also the initial Viewpoint and Focus. We structure that space with the information that Max is twenty-three years old.

(2) Keeping that space in Focus, we add the (present) information that Max has lived abroad. This information is presented via a past Event space ("Max live abroad").

(3) In the next sentence, *in 1990* is a space builder. It sets up a new Focus space, in which we build the content "Max live in Rome." This is also the new Event space, as we are considering the event/state of Max living in Rome.

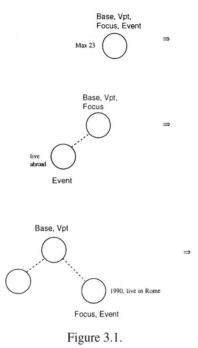

Figure 3.1.

(4) This Focus space now becomes a Viewpoint from which to consider Max's next move. Intuitively, when we say *In 1991, he would
move ...,* we are presenting 1991 as a future with respect to 1990.
The 1990 space ("Max in Rome") becomes a Viewpoint from which to
set up the next Focus (and Event) space, 1991, with the content "Max
move to Venice." We could have said the "same" thing differently by
using the Base (present time) as a Viewpoint: *In 1991, Max moved to
Venice.*

(5) The last sentence, *He would then have lived a year in Rome,* keeps
1990 as the Viewpoint, and 1991 as the Focus, while using an Event
space ("live a year in Rome") that is past time relative to the Focus
1991.

Schematically, the space configuration develops with successive shifts
of Event, Focus, and Viewpoint as shown in Figs. 3.1 and 3.2. The virtue
of this type of cognitive organization is to allow local manipulation of
the spaces without losing sight of the entire configuration. As time is the
relevant dimension here, we need some indication of the time relationship between spaces. Typically, tense will provide us with indications of

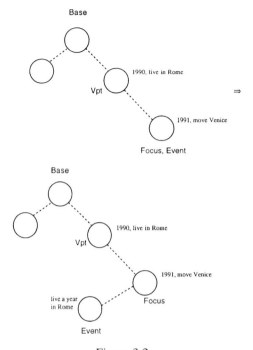

Figure 3.2.

relative time relationship. Cutrer (1994) proposes putatively universal semantic tense-aspect categories, with language-specific means of expressing some of their combinations. She also introduces a crucial distinction: New structure introduced into spaces may be marked as FACT or as PREDICTION, depending on the semantic tense-aspect.

Let us start by looking at the three basic semantic tense categories PAST, PRESENT, FUTURE. Here is the mental-space characterization provided by Cutrer for each one:

PAST applied to space N indicates that:

(1) N is in Focus
(2) N's parent is Viewpoint
(3) N's time is prior to Viewpoint (i.e., prior to N's parent)
(4) events or properties represented in N are FACT (in relation to the parent Viewpoint space)

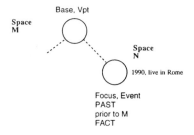

Figure 3.3.

In our example, PAST is indicated by the English past tense of the verb *lived (in 1990, he lived in Rome); in 1990* is a space builder that sets up a space N from the Base (its parent). PAST (marked here by the English *-ed*) indicates (1) that N is now the Focus space; (2) that N's parent (the Base space in this example) is the Viewpoint; (3) that N's time, namely 1990, is prior to the Base time (perhaps the time of speech); and (4) that events in N (Max's living in Rome) are presented as FACT. This expresses, of course, a simple local relation. As we shall see, the power of the overall system driving discourse dynamics comes from the combinatorial possibilities afforded by the mechanisms as shown in Fig. 3.3.

PRESENT applied to N indicates that:

(1)   N is in Focus
(2)   N or N's parent is Viewpoint
(3)   the time frame represented in N is *not* prior to Viewpoint/Base
(4)   events or properties in N are FACT (with respect to Viewpoint)

In our simple example, PRESENT (English present tense *Max is twenty-three*) is applied to the Base, Viewpoint, Max's age is presented as FACT in the Base, and the property ("twenty-three years old") holds at Base time (e.g., speech time) and beyond (see Fig. 3.4).

As we shall see, this characterization allows for more elaborate combinations in which PRESENT is not the time of speech. Cutrer (1994) cites the following types:

The train leaves tomorrow at 4. [future events considered factual]
French people eat escargots. [generic]
On Tuesday, John sees a therapist. [habitual]

Figure 3.4.

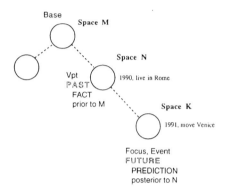

Figure 3.5.

First you cook the meat, then you add the vegetables. ["timeless"
  recipes, instructions]
*I walk into this bar last night and this guy comes up to me, and he says
  . . .*[historical present—involves a shift in Base space]
If it <u>rains</u> tomorrow, I will buy an umbrella. [hypothetical space]

FUTURE applied to space K indicates that:

(1)   K is in Focus
(2)   K's parent is Viewpoint
(3)   the time frame for K is posterior to Viewpoint
(4)   events or properties in K are PREDICTION (from Viewpoint)

In the example of Max moving to Venice, FUTURE is applied to the
space set up by *in 1991*. When that space is constructed in the discourse,
the current Viewpoint is the space *1990* (Max living in Rome). The
event of Max moving to Venice is presented from that viewpoint as a
PREDICTION, posterior to the time frame of *1990* as in Fig. 3.5. In order
to reflect this dynamic process, language retraces the path from the Base

to the Focus space by means of grammatical tenses. In English, we find the following system:

PAST is coded by the simple past (*lived, went, brought*), or by *have + past participle* if it is in infinitival position (*will have forgotten, may have left, claims to have forgotten*). Code: verb + past or *have +* (verb + *past participle*)
FUTURE is coded by *will +* verb.

Now, in our example, when the sentence *In 1991, he would move to Venice* comes into the discourse, K is the Focus/Event space, N (1990) is the Viewpoint space, and M is the Base. The grammatical coding reflects the path followed from the Base to the Focus:

Base Space M   ---PAST---> Viewpoint Space N

--- FUTURE----> Focus Space K

The coding will appear on the verb *move* that is bringing structure into Focus Space K:

Simple past + [*will* + Verb *move*]

⇒   (past + *will*) + *move*

⇒   *would move*

In this way, the grammatical information allows us to reconstruct the path followed from the Base, with shifts in Viewpoint and Focus. It allows speaker and hearer to represent the overall time relations between events, and their status as Fact or Prediction, because although the operations are local, the overall configuration is available, and the path is traced back to the Base, not just to the immediate parent of the Focus space. Notice that absolute time relations are not given by the language here. We do not know from the space configuration whether 1991 (Space K) is prior or posterior to the Base (Space M). We only know that K is after N, and that N is before M. Of course, extra information can be available pragmatically. If we know that Base time = Speech time = 1994, we will assume that Max did in fact move to Venice. K is then prior to M, and although it has only a PREDICTION status from Viewpoint N, it can acquire a FACT status from a different Viewpoint (in this case M).

Suppose now that our minidiscourse contained:

In 1990 he lived in Rome. In 1989, he had left New York.

The space builder *in 1989* sets up a space H, prior to N. The Time Path from the Base is:

Base M ---PAST ---> Space N ---PAST ---> Space H

The grammar will mark this path on the verb *leave* in the Focus Space H. The coding of the first PAST is simple past, as before. The coding of the second one is *have* + past participle, because it is embedded under the first (grammatically in infinitival position). The combination that codes the Time Path will therefore be:

simple past + [*have* + [verb *leave* + past participle]]

$\Rightarrow$ (past + *have*) + (*leave* + past participle)

$\Rightarrow$ (*had*) + (*left*)

$\Rightarrow$ had left

Of course, languages have different ways of coding the Time Path, and grammar may highlight some aspects of the path, while underspecifying others. A common way of marking FUTURE is by means of a future inflectional ending. Inflections may in turn combine morphologically. For example, a FUTURE Time Path from the Base will be coded as follows in French for the verb *partir* ("leave") in space K:

Time Path: Base Space M (Viewpoint) - - -FUTURE- - - -> Space K (Focus)

coding: verb + future inflection

partir + future

$\Rightarrow$ *partir-a* (3rd person sing.)

If, as in our English example, the FUTURE was applied to K from a Viewpoint that is itself PAST with respect to the Base, the Time Path would be marked by a different inflection:

En 1991, Max partirait à Venise. ["In 1991, Max would leave for Venice."]

Base M - - -PAST- - - -> Viewpoint N - - -FUTURE- - - -> Focus K

coding: past + (future + verb *partir*)

$\rightarrow$ *partir* + past future inflection

$\Rightarrow$ *partir-ait* (3d person sing.)

Now let us consider some additional tense/aspect categories. In his important book *Partitioned Representations* (1991), Dinsmore shows that the PERFECT sets up a new mental space but does not shift Focus. Accordingly, Cutrer defines PERFECT as follows:

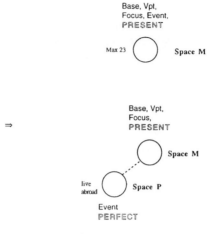

Figure 3.6.

PERFECT applies to an Event space N and indicates that

    (1)   N is not in Focus
    (2)   N's parent is Viewpoint
    (3)   N's time is prior to Viewpoint

In our example, we have two PERFECTs. The first is coded by the sentence *He has lived abroad.* A prior event is referred to in order to highlight a present property of Max (being someone who has lived abroad). The Base space remains Viewpoint and Focus, but Event shifts to a new space. Dynamically, the evolution of the configuration is shown in Fig. 3.6. English codes the PERFECT with:

have + verb + past participle

The Time Path for our example is:

PRESENT Base Space M ---PERFECT----> Event Space P

The coding in English of this Time Path is:

Present tense + [*have* + verb *live* + past participle]

= [*have* + pres] + [*live* + pp]

= *has lived*

Now consider the minidiscourse once again:

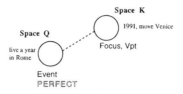

Figure 3.7.

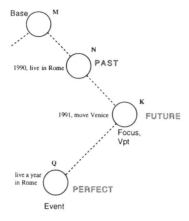

Figure 3.8.

Max is twenty-three. He has lived abroad. In 1990, he lived in Rome. In 1991 he would move to Venice. He would then have lived a year in Rome.

The last sentence also contains a perfect ("having lived a year in Rome"). Locally, an Event space is set up at a stage in the discourse where the Focus space is K ("moving to Venice, 1991"). It is from the Viewpoint of this Focus space K that we access the Event space Q ("live a year in Rome") (see Fig. 3.7).

PERFECT establishes a local link between spaces K and Q. The constraint is that K become Viewpoint, remain in Focus, and be posterior in time to Q. In the sentence that structures Q (*He would then have lived a year in Rome*), the Time Path is coded all the way back to the Base space. The relevant subpart of the configuration at that point (Time Path from M to Q) is shown in Fig. 3.8. The Time Path from the Base is therefore:

Base M ---PAST----> Space N ---FUTURE----> Vpt, Focus K

   ---PERFECT----> Event Space Q

The English coding applies compositionally to reflect this Time Path:

simple past tense + [*will* + [*have* + [verb *live* + past participle]]]

⇒   [*will* + past] + [*have* + [*live* + pp]]

⇒   *would* + [*have lived*]

⇒   *would have lived*

Languages differ, of course, in the type of coding they adopt and what they code. The general devices are auxiliaries (like *will* and *have*) and verb forms (past participle, future inflection, etc.). French, for example, has a special verb inflection (*conditional*) for the Time Subpath "Space ---PAST----> Space ---FUTURE----> Space." The PERFECT is coded as in English, with *avoir* ("have") + verb + past participle. Accordingly, the Time Path we just examined (for the English sentence *He would then have lived a year in Rome*):

Base M ---PAST---->Space N ---FUTURE----> Vpt, Focus K

                                                        ---PERFECT---->Event Space Q

would be coded as:

            (past + future) + [*avoir* + [verb *habiter* + past participle]]

⇒   (*avoir* + conditional) + (*habiter* + past participle)

⇒   *aurait habité*

The point of these examples is that English and French are coding the same semantic discourse Time Path from the Base to the Event space, even though the grammatical sequences look superficially different.

Codings can be ambiguous. In English, the coding is the same in infinitival position for the PAST and for the PERFECT. This means the English present perfect will be distinguished from the English simple past, but PAST PAST and PAST PERFECT will have the same coding:

He has lived in Venice.
*Last year, he has lived in Venice.
Last year, he lived in Venice.

As shown by Dinsmore (1991), the sentence **Last year, he has lived in Venice* is ungrammatical because the space builder *last year* indicates that the space is in Focus, while the present perfect tells us that the space is PERFECT, and therefore not in Focus. English distinguishes between

PERFECT and PAST in this case. But if an extra "layer" of PAST or FUTURE
is added, that distinction will be lost:

He had lived in Venice. (PAST + PERFECT)
The year before, he had lived in Venice. (PAST + PAST)

The Time Paths represent a dynamic unfolding of discourse. The tense
combinations are not meaning properties of single sentences or propo-
sitions. They are codings of the discourse configuration into which the
sentence fits. It is crucial for this scheme that Viewpoint, Focus, Event,
and even Base be reassigned as discourse unfolds. Cutrer (1994) provides the principles of discourse organization that regulate the shifts and
the successive assignments. I refer the reader to her work for a complete
and careful exposition of these principles. They include constraints of
the following type:

- There can be only one Focus and one Base at any given moment of the
  discourse interpretation;
- new spaces are built from Base or Focus;
- Focus can shift to Event, Base, or previous Focus;
- Viewpoint can shift to Focus or Base.

For instance, in a continuation of the Rome and Venice example,
Viewpoint could shift back to the Base while space K (1991) remained
in Focus. K would now be accessed directly from the Base instead of
from N, and the Time Path would be:

> Base, Viewpoint Space M - - -PAST- - - -> Focus Space K

A sentence expressing this would be:

In 1991, Max explored all the canals and fell in love

where *explored* and *fell* are in the simple past, corresponding to the new
Time Path. At that point, the entire discourse configuration would look
as in Fig. 3.9.

1.2. Sequence of Tense

The language-specific coding mechanisms for local connections between spaces are ultimately responsible, through their reapplication and
combination, for the surface distributions of verbal forms. Some of these
combinations are very frequent and typical. They are often reflected
in the rules proposed by school grammars. Others are rare, or at least

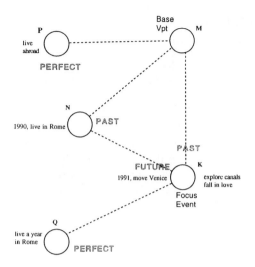

Figure 3.9.

untypical, because they correspond to less likely space configurations. We look in this section at some aspects of grammatical distributions.

In English, hypotheticals of the form *If A, then B* set up two successive spaces, a Foundation H and an Expansion J.[1] So the sentence *If Alberta is in Canada, then Calgary is in North America* first sets up a space H, hypothetical with respect to the Base. In H, "Alberta is in Canada," J is an Expansion of H: it inherits H's explicit structure as background and acquires extra explicit structure of its own corresponding to "Calgary is in North America." Importantly, explicit information in H is presented as FACT. Because the structure is hypothetical, we know that this information is not factual relative to the Base. It is construed as factual only within the hypothetical subconfiguration. This is intuitively very similar to what happens when we place ourselves fictively in a situation construed as factual:

Suppose that it rains tomorrow. Then we will stay in the house.

In the fictive situation, tomorrow's rain is a premise. It is taken to be a given fact. Given that fact, other aspects of the situation are built up, either as PREDICTION (*we shall ...*), or as FACT (*...Then we stay in the house*). This construal is reflected by the grammar. Even though the time of the hypothetical event is posterior to now, the present tense

1. See Chapter 5.

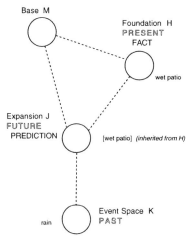

Figure 3.10.

is used, just as in the case of *The boat leaves tomorrow at noon*. This is because PRESENT as a semantic tense/aspect category indicates a time *non-prior* to Base, and a construal of events as FACT. In the "*if... then ...*" construction, we find exactly the same tense distribution:

If it rains tomorrow, we will stay in the house.

The premise is construed as FACT. The consequence can be construed as PREDICTION. And if so, the time of the Expansion space (consequences) is computed relative to the Base. This is essentially the scheme proposed by Cutrer. It explains the superficially paradoxical sequence of tenses found in these conditionals: a present in the protasis (even if the time is future), followed by a future in the apodosis (even if that time is the same as in the protasis). Consider also:

If the patio is wet tomorrow night, it will have rained during the day.

The time of the hypothetical fact ("wet patio") is posterior to the Base time, and posterior to the events of the Expansion ("rain during the day"). This example shows that the reference time for the Expansion is actually the same as for the Foundation. The expression *will have rained* indicates a Time Path going first to "tomorrow night" (FUTURE) and then back in time to "during the day" (PAST—*have rained*).

The overall space configuration must therefore be as shown in Fig. 3.10. Notice that in this configuration, the Time Path for K goes directly from

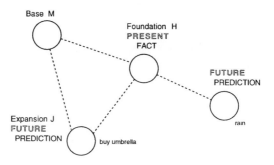

Figure 3.11.

the Base to the Expansion, bypassing H. This is reflected by the super-ficially anomalous sequence of tenses. Configurations of this type are used for reasoning via the operation of Matching, which we will study in Chapter 5.

We can understand them more intuitively in the following way. The Foundation space H builds up additional background structure, just like the one in the initial Base. The Expansion space J is constructed on the basis of this additional background (factual) structure and the original Base. The partitioning keeps the Base and the Foundation dis-tinct, so that we keep track of what is "real" and what is "hypothetical." But for the Expansion, it is as if the Base were the combination (the "blend," in the terms of Chapter 6) of M and H.

As Fillmore (1990) and Dancygier and Sweetser (1996) have ob-served, it is quite possible to get a future tense in the "*if. . .*" clause (protasis) of the conditional, but with a different meaning:

[context: the weather service announces that it will rain tomorrow]
If it will rain tomorrow, then we will buy an umbrella today.

As Dancygier and Sweetser show, this is an epistemic use. What we set up as a hypothetical fact is not tomorrow's rain, but rather the current prediction that there will *be* rain. It is not tomorrow's rain that makes us buy an umbrella today (we can't go back in time). Rather, it is the prediction today of tomorrow's rain that makes us buy the umbrella. In this case, what appears in the Foundation H happens to be itself a future prediction as given in Fig. 3.11. Because there is more than one possible Time Path to access a particular space, there will be more than one way to say "the same thing." And there will be different Sequence of Tense possibilities for them. So consider another one of Cutrer's examples:

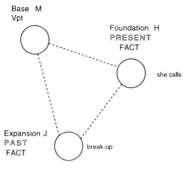

Figure 3.12.

If she calls, then she broke up with her boyfriend.

This is what Sweetser (1990) calls an epistemic conditional. It is not the phone call that causes the breakup. Rather, it is the truth of *she calls* that allows one to infer the truth of *she broke up.* The hypothetical posterior fact is set up in a Foundation space and displayed by means of the English present tense (reflecting its status as FACT and not prior to the Base). The Expansion ("breakup") is prior to the Base, and also construed as FACT. The Time Path is computed from the Base: the breakup, *if it occurred,* is prior to Base time. The configuration is given in Fig. 3.12.

What prevents structure in space J from being interpreted as ordinary factual information relative to the Base is that J is linked, and subordinate, to the *hypothetical* space H. Any space subordinate to H is in the hypothetical domain. As explained in more detail in Chapter 5, this is a matching configuration: If, in the dynamic evolution of discourse, space M (the Base) comes to match H, then the Expansion J will be fully incorporated in M.

A sentence very close in meaning to the one just examined would be:

If she calls, she will have broken up with her boyfriend.

The Time Path here is different from the previous one. The Expansion space, this time, is cotemporal with the Foundation. We take as a new Viewpoint the time when she called. From that Viewpoint, we go back in time to the "breakup" (see Fig. 3.13). This configuration presents the "breakup" as taking place before the (hypothetical) phone call. We cannot tell from the grammar alone whether it is prior or posterior to the

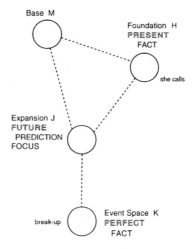

Figure 3.13.

Base. This is unspecified by the expression itself, but might of course be recoverable from other pragmatic knowledge.

Grammarians and linguists often attempt to rule out certain sequences of tenses on syntactic grounds by specifying formally which sequences are allowable. A deeper explanation is that the tense sequence reflects a Time Path between spaces, and that some Time Paths are frequent and typical, others unlikely but possible, and others impossible. Cutrer takes the following sentences, which sound ill-formed in isolation (i.e., with minimal context), and provides short discourses in which they all code acceptable Time Paths:

If she has the baby in June, then she had gotten pregnant. [PAST PERF]
If she has the baby in June, then she will have gotten pregnant (. . .).
   [FUT PERF]
If she has the baby in June, then she would have gotten pregnant (. . .).
   [PAST FUT PERF]
If she has the baby in June, then it would be her husband's child. [PAST
   FUT]

1.3. Verbs of Speech

An especially interesting area studied by Cutrer is the Time Paths created by speech verbs. Speech verbs set up spaces partitioning out the content of what is said, and these speech spaces have the following important special properties:

• They have an inherent strong Viewpoint Role filled by the speaker or experiencer of the reported speech event.
• The Speech Space represents a time period that minimally includes the time of the reported speech event (but may be larger).
    The Speech Space and all spaces subordinate to it constitute a *Speech Domain*. A configuration containing a Speech Domain has two inherent Viewpoints, the one from the Base, and one from the Speech Space.
• Spaces in the Speech Domain are assigned a FACT or PREDICTION status with respect to the Speech Space.
• Spaces in the Speech Domain may be accessed via the following access paths:
    —directly from the Speech Space;
    —directly from the Base;
    —from the Base via the Speech Space.

Here are some of Cutrer's examples for these possible access paths:

Directly from the Speech Space
John will announce at midnight that he <u>burned</u> the documents two hours before.

The speech event (John's announcement) is posterior to Base, and has the status PREDICTION (*will announce*). Speech space S (content of announcement) has the time of the announcement. Space T ("burn documents") is prior to S. The event in T is marked by a verb (*burned*) in the simple past, although it is in fact posterior in time to the Base and not FACT with respect to the Base. This is because the access is directly from the Speech Space: from the point of view of John announcing the event, the burning is FACT and *prior* to S, as shown in Fig. 3.14.

The important property of these configurations is that the coding of the Time Path does not need to go all the way back to the Base; it can be started at the Speech Space. In fact, we cannot use the Time Path from the Base in this case, as that would be:

BASE ---FUTURE----> M -----> S ---PAST----> T

which would be coded as:

will + [have + [burn + past participle]] = will have burned

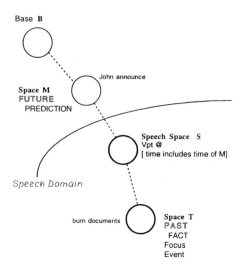

Figure 3.14.

yielding the ungrammatical sentence:

**John will announce at midnight that he will have burned the
documents two hours before.*

Cutrer shows that this path is disallowed because it marks as PRE-
DICTION (with *will*) an event which is FACT from the Speech Space
Viewpoint (the event "burn the documents"). This clash of FACT with
PREDICTION is systematically disallowed. If there is no such clash, then
the two Time Paths are permitted. We have:

*Tom announced at midnight that he burned the documents two hours
before.* [same Time Path as above: directly from Speech Space]
or

From Base via Speech Space

*Tom announced at midnight that he had burned the documents two
hours before.*

Time Path all the way back to the Base:

BASE ---PAST----> M ------> Speech S ---PAST----> Event T

coding: Simple past + [*have* + verb *burn* + past participle] = *had burned*

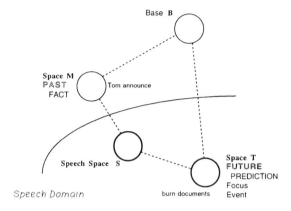

Figure 3.15.

Directly from Base

Finally, it is possible to access a space in the Speech Domain directly from the Base, without going through the Speech Space:

Tom will announce next month that he <u>burned</u> the documents last week.
Tom announced yesterday that he <u>will burn</u> the documents tomorrow.

Compare with *Tom announced yesterday that he <u>would</u> burn the documents tomorrow,* where the Time Path does go through the Speech Space:

BASE ---PAST---> M, S ---FUTURE--> T)

Direct Access from the Base corresponds to the configuration is shown in Fig. 3.15. The space T that we find here is also necessarily FUTURE with respect to the Speech Space S, because S is prior to the Base. T is assigned PREDICTION status with respect to S and there is no clash: T has the same status (PREDICTION) with respect to Base and Speech Space.

However, if the status is not the same, and there is a clash between FACT and PREDICTION, then Cutrer shows—and this is a deep result— that the configuration is ruled out. So, for example, *Jack said that he was sick* has two time interpretations: one in which the sickness is prior to Jack's speech, and one in which the sickness is cotemporal with the speech event. The first interpretation corresponds to a Time Path originating in the Speech Space, and coded by Simple Past (*was sick*). The other interpretation corresponds to a Time Path directly from the Base to the Focus Space, also coded by the Simple Past. The Focus Space is assigned FACT status from the Speech Space and from the Base.

There is no clash. In contrast, *Jack will say that he will be sick* does *not* admit a cotemporal interpretation: The announced sickness can only be posterior to the saying. This is because on the cotemporal reading, from Jack's Viewpoint, the sickness would be FACT, whereas from the Base, it would be PREDICTION (marked by *will*). This clash is outlawed. The cotemporal interpretation must be expressed by means of a different Time Path:

Jack will say that he is sick.

The Time Path originates in the Speech Space, is coded by the present tense, and assigns the status FACT to the Focus Space ("Jack sick"). This status FACT is of course relative to the Speech Space.

Notice that, as the time frame for PRESENT is defined as non-prior to Base, we don't get

Jack said last year that he is sick

with the interpretation that he was sick last year. Nor can we get a reading where he was announcing last year that he would be sick today. This would constitute a FACT/PREDICTION clash. The interpretation we can get is that his sickness extends over a period including the time when he spoke and Base time. The following examples make the same point:

Jack told us last year that he knows Latin.
Jack said yesterday that he has the flu.

If, on the other hand, the event is posterior to Base time but construed as FACT from both Viewpoints (Base and Speech), then the present tense is appropriate, as expected:

Jack told us yesterday that his train leaves this afternoon at five.

For the same reason, if today is March 15, we don't get:

Jack said on January 29 that he will leave on February 10

because the future marker *will* is in the present tense, precluding an event time (February 10) prior to Base (March 15). The Time Path we must use goes from Base to Speech to Focus (PAST, FUTURE), coded by the English form *would leave*. The simple future, corresponding to the Time Path (PRESENT, FUTURE) is fine if the Focus time is later than March 15:

Jack said on January 29 that he will leave on April 1.

Finally, consider the following simple situation. Today is March 15, 1995. On November 1, 1994, Jack said, "On January 1, 1995, I will burn the documents," and indeed he did burn them on New Year's day. Why can't his announcement be reported as:

Jack said last year that he burned the documents on January 1 of this year.

The past tense would indicate correctly that the burning is, and was announced to be, prior to March 15. The reason this doesn't work is, once again, Cutrer's FACT/PREDICTION principle: The burning has PREDICTION status from the Speech Viewpoint and FACT status from the Base Viewpoint. This clash is ruled out. In contrast, if Jack had announced an event that already had FACT status from his Speech Viewpoint, the sequence of tenses would be fine:

Jack said on November 1, 1994, that his boat left on January 1, 1995.[2]

1.4. Epistemic Distance

The general function of tense is to mark local distance between mental spaces along certain dimensions. The most prominent of these dimensions is time, but perhaps equally important is the dimension of epistemic distance. When a conditional space is set up, the speaker can mark the degree to which the "hypothesis" made in that space is likely or unlikely to hold in its parent space. In English, the past tense is a general distal form which can be used to mark prior time, but also greater epistemic distance. Compare:

If you go fishing tomorrow, you will have food for me.
If you went fishing tomorrow, you would have food for me.

The two examples do not differ with respect to the events described or with respect to their time of occurrence. They differ only in the status of the hypothetical premise of your going fishing. The first example is neutral: We don't know whether you'll go fishing or not. The second takes a negative stance toward the event, and may be used even if we know that

2. Cf. *Jack said that he burned the documents*. From the Base, it is not established or predicted that he in fact burned them. In the same way, for the text example, we don't know whether the boat actually left on January 1. We only know that Jack presented it as a scheduled event.

you are not going fishing. It is then interpreted as a counterfactual. In both cases, a hypothetical mental space is constructed, but the tense is used to specify not its time relation to its parent, but rather its epistemic distance.

As Sweetser (1996) shows, the past tense marking epistemic distance will spread to all spaces subordinate to the hypothetical one:

If you have Triple-A, then if you go to a telephone, you can solve your problem.

If you had Triple-A, then if you went to a telephone, you could solve your problem.

If you had had Triple-A, then if you had gone to a phone, you could have solved your problem.

The past tenses of *went* and *could* in the second example are triggered by the past tense marking (negative stance) in the highest hypothetical space (*if you had Triple-A*). The third example contains verb forms with two past tenses each. One reflects prior time, the other reflects epistemic distance and strongly suggests counterfactuality—that "you, in fact, did not have Triple-A." The double past tense marking applies to all the forms, because the corresponding events are all in the scope of the hypothetical with negative stance and prior time (*if you had had Triple-A*).

Another way to state this is as a generalization on space tracking. The coding system is indifferent to the type of distance (time or epistemic) marked between spaces. It applies all the way from the Base (or the Speech space) in a perfectly regular way, and the tenses combine compositionally without regard for the type of distance being coded.

Sweetser shows that this holds generally for constructions embedded in *if*-conditionals:

If we ate subtraction stew, then the more we <u>ate</u>, the hungrier we <u>would get</u>.

If we had eaten subtraction stew, then the more we<u>'d've</u> eaten, the hungrier we<u>'d've</u> gotten.[3]

There are further interesting and intriguing aspects of epistemic stance and distance phenomena that I will not pursue here. Extensive discussions

---

3. The third example is counterfactual and, in addition to the double past, we find the equivalent of a conditional mood in the embedded construction, marked by "*'d*," a contracted form of *would*.

and analyses can be found in Fillmore (1990), Sweetser (1996), and Cutrer (1994, chap. 5).

2. Mood

Mood (indicative, subjunctive, optative, conditional, . . .) is another powerful, universal grammatical means of keeping track of mental-space configurations and access paths. The ways in which languages use mood for this purpose are exceedingly complex and diverse, and I will not attempt, in this book, to deal with the topic. But a few examples, including some from Mejías-Bikandi's perspicuous study of mental-space accessibility in Spanish, may give an idea of the mechanisms and subtleties involved.

A well-known class of space builders, verbs corresponding to *want, wish, not believe, doubt,* and so on mark the explicit content of the mental spaces they introduce with the subjunctive in languages like French. If elements are introduced directly into such spaces by means of descriptions containing relative clauses, a subjunctive may (or must) be used in that relative clause, whereas if the element is accessed from a higher space, the indicative is typically used.

*Max voudrait que tu achètes une voiture qui **soit** rapide.*

				SUBJ		SUBJ
Max	want	you	buy	a car that		be fast.

[Max has no specific car in mind; he just wants whatever car you buy to be fast.]

*Max voudrait que tu achètes une voiture qui **est** rapide.*

				SUBJ		INDIC

[Max has in mind a specific car or make of car.]

The choice of mood in such cases constrains the Access path by indicating in which space the description holds.

In a similar way, the conditional mood in French is used to signal the type of space that "we are in." Strong and weak counterfactuals typically set up their Foundation Space as FACT with an indicative in the protasis of an *if. . . then* . . . construction. The Expansion Space[4] is then signaled grammatically by the conditional mood.

4. See Chapter 5 for more on Foundation and Expansion Spaces. For *If A, then B,*" the Foundation corresponds to the matching conditions set up by the protasis (antecedent) clause *A*. The Expansion corresponds to the elaboration of the hypothetical space by *B*, and other sentences that may follow and will be in the same mood as *B*.

Si tu venais demain, tu serais content. Tu t'amuserais beaucoup.
  INDIC   COND   COND
if you came tomorrow, you would   you would have a lot of fun
        be pleased

A different but related use of the conditional is the journalistic device of using this mood to indicate information that is not firmly established. Such information is thus confined to a space that is distanced from the Base.

*Le président **aurait rencontré** secrètement les chefs rebelles.*
          COND
The president "would have" secretly met with the rebel leaders.
[It is said/rumored that the president met secretly with the rebel leaders.]

Mejías-Bikandi (1996) shows in much greater detail how the choice of mood constrains the accessibility of mental spaces in Spanish. Consider first the following contrast.

*Tal vez su hijo **está** en la cárcel.*
       INDIC
*Tal vez su hijo **esté** en la cárcel.*
       SUBJ
Maybe his son is in jail.

The space builder *tal vez* sets up a possibility space relative to the Base. In that space, the definite description *su hijo* introduces a presupposition that "he" has a son. The difference between the two forms is the following. The first with the indicative allows the presupposition to float up to the Base; it is assumed that "he" actually does have a son. The second form, with the subjunctive, limits the accessibility. The presupposition does not float up; "he" may or may not actually have a son.

Similarly, there are two ways of saying "It is not the case that the unions have stopped supporting the government."

*No es cierto que los sindicatos **han** dejado de apoyar al gobierno.*
                    INDIC
*No es cierto que los sindicatos **hayan** dejado de apoyar al gobierno.*
                    SUBJ

"Stopped supporting" introduces the presupposition (in the subordinate counterfactual space) that the unions used to support the government. The first sentence (indicative), but not the second (subjunctive), lets the presupposition float up to the Base. The subjunctive form leaves open the possibility that the unions never supported the government in the first place.

Mejías-Bikandi shows that Space-Accessibility, as constrained by the choice of mood for the embedded space, will entail differences in the availability of dicourse referents. The following two sentences both mean "I don't think I have shown you a picture of my parents."

No creo que te <u>he</u> enseñado una foto de mis padres.
           INDIC
No creo que te <u>haya</u> enseñado una foto de mis padres.
           SUBJ

The first naturally sets up *una foto*, the picture, as specific—that is, accessed from the Base and available as a later discourse referent ("here <u>it</u> is"). The second form (subjunctive) has a strongly preferred interpretation where the photo is nonspecific. That is, the corresponding mental-space element is introduced directly into the subordinate space; accessibility to the Base is restricted.

Mejías-Bikandi provides a wide array of other examples and additional data, and draws the following general conclusion:

The observations and the representations given above point to the following generalization. Informally, the indicative mood opens a space M, allowing elements within M to be linked to elements in a higher space, or allowing presuppositions within M to be inherited in a higher space. On the other hand, the use of the subjunctive mood closes a space M to such relations, so that elements within M cannot be linked to elements in a higher space, and presuppositions within M are not typically inherited.

Another extremely interesting piece of work on space accessibility in Spanish is Doiz-Bienzobas (1995, chap. 5). Doiz-Bienzobas shows that the imperfect, as opposed to the preterite, renders accessible embedded perception spaces, quantifier spaces, irrealis and movie spaces. The choice of aspect allows a shift of viewpoint to embedded spaces. Thus the choice of the imperfect is another space-tracking device, allowing participants to identify accessible viewpoint spaces and to figure out which space in a configuration is in the process of receiving additional structure.

The general view developed in this chapter concerning Tense and Mood is that, although they have important consequences for the content of what is expressed, their primary cognitive function is to allow speaker and listeners to keep track of the everchanging dynamics of mental-space configurations. As it turns out, the track-keeping mechanisms that natural languages have developed are extremely intricate and sophisticated. The language mechanisms we have seen, important in their own right, also give us incomparable insight into deeper cognitive aspects of the ways in which we manage ongoing flows of information. The concepts of Viewpoint, Focus, Anchoring, and Accessibility are an integral part of general cognition.

Chapter 4
Analogical Counterfactuals

How does language tie in with reasoning? One reasonable and fairly widespread view is that sentences yield meanings and that such meanings can serve as input to higher-level forms of reasoning like deduction, induction, and analogy. Under that view, the important function of language is to provide information that can be exploited by the reasoning processes, for example premises for a deductive argument or the specification of a structure that will be used analogically.

Research in cognitive linguistics supports a different conception. Language is actively involved in setting up construals, mappings between domains, and discourse configurations, with the fundamental properties of Accessing, Spreading, and Viewpoint. The formal properties that we find at the most basic semantic/pragmatic level of meaning construction are the same as the ones found in general reasoning, narrative structure, and other high-level forms of thinking and communication. The mental operations that allow us to construct meanings for the simple-looking words and sentences of our everyday life are the same ones at work in what we recognize more consciously as creative thought and expression.

A clear example of the hidden unity of micro- and macro-meaning construction processes can be found in counterfactual phenomena. The importance of such phenomena has long been recognized. To quote from Nelson Goodman's seminal article written in 1947: "The analysis of counterfactual conditionals is no fussy little grammatical exercise. Indeed, if we lack the means for interpreting counterfactual conditionals, we can hardly claim to have any adequate philosophy of science."

What Goodman pointed to were hidden logical complexities in commonly used sentences like (1):

A version of this chapter has been published as a separate article in Fauconnier and Sweetser (1996). I wish to thank the University of Chicago Press for permission to use the essay "Analogical Counterfactuals" from *Spaces, Worlds, and Grammar* (©1996 by the University of Chicago, all rights reserved).

(1) *If that piece of butter had been heated to 150°F, it would have
     melted.*

His work started a long and interesting tradition of developing a logical
semantics that might accommodate such expressions and overcome a
host of noted difficulties.[1] Counterfactuals are typically associated with
the kind of grammatical construction exemplified in (1), although, as we
shall see, they show up in other guises as well. Here are some typical
examples of forms that have received attention:

(2) *If we were on the beach, we would be having fun.*
(3) *If I had been Reagan, I wouldn't have sold arms to Iran.*
(4) *If I was a writer (who votes for the Cy Young) and looking at the
     numbers and how the pitchers have performed throughout the
     year, I would say I would be the leader.* [pitcher Saberhagen, a
     Kansas City right-hander, in an interview]
(5) *If the tau lepton had existed in the 1 GEV range, I would have
     discovered it.* [disappointed physicist Zichichi]
(6) *If all circles were large, and this small triangle Δ were a circle,
     would it be large?* [example from Moser (1988)]

Several different techniques have been applied to such examples, but
in most cases the spirit of the approach has been essentially this: A
counterfactual sets up an imaginary situation that differs from the actual
one in one fundamental respect, expressed in the antecedent part *A* (the
"protasis") of the *if A then B* construction. Its meaning consists in linking
the apodosis *B* to this imaginary situation, as a consequence: Change
the world just enough to make *A* true, and *B* will also be true.[2] As it
turns out, this is easier said than done. The change produced by making
A true instead of false typically ripples through the entire situation,
and it is a formidable problem to characterize what is and what is not
immune to change in trying to build the counterfactual situation. Take,
for example, sentence (2) above, and assume (*a*) *that people always
have fun on the beach, except when it rains,* (*b*) *that "we" are currently
not having fun* and (*c*) *that it is not raining.* The understanding of (2) is
based on preserving (*c*) and changing (*b*) as a consequence of *being on
the beach* plus (*a*) and (*c*). One could just as well, however, preserve (*b*)
and abandon (*c*), which would yield the counterfactual:

1. For an excellent critical review of this tradition, along with some original proposals, see Brée
   1982. Detailed logical accounts are developed, for example, in Lewis 1973 and Goldstick 1978.
   Important linguistic treatments of the counterpart problem and world-creating predicates are
   found in McCawley 1981 and Morgan 1973.
2. *B* may already be true in the actual situation.

(7) *If we were on the beach, it would be raining.*

But this statement, in contrast with (2), does not sound like a natural one to make in the chosen context. As Goodman observed, the logically possible changes from the actual to the imagined situation, when *A* is assumed, are not equal candidates for computing the counterfactual.

Suppose, however, that this obstacle could be overcome, that we could systematically find the intended imaginary situation from which *B* is deemed to follow.[3] Would that tell us what the expression means? It would not, because the imaginary situation would still not be linked to reality, and the consequences to be drawn would not appear. For instance, having the minimum change from actuality that would replace Reagan by myself, and having ascertained that in such a situation arms would not be sold to Iran, what could we conclude about the actual situation? How could this fanciful invention entail the sort of thing it typically does, for instance, that I disapprove of the arms sale, or of Reagan, or that I am proud of my high moral standards, or that I wish I could come up with smart ideas like Reagan's, and so on. Well, that's pragmatics, some will say, and indeed it is—but the counterfactual story is pointless if we don't know how to link it to the intended meaning. We need to know what the point of constructing an alternative situation is: What does the alternative situation have to say about the one we're in?

As it turns out, Goodman's problem and the pragmatic issue are linked. In spite of appearances, the structure of counterfactuals is not truth-functional (entailment from an alternative set of premises); it is analogical—projection of structure from one domain to another. The theoretical import of these characteristics is significant: Expressions of natural languages are best viewed as maximally economical means of triggering complex projection of structures across discourse domains (here, mental spaces). This fundamental feature of language and thought, neglected in traditional accounts,[4] ties in very nicely with contemporary research on the role of metaphorical mappings in core semantics,[5] the extraction of abstract schemas in semantic construction,[6] the analysis

---

3. As pointed out in Goldstick 1978, Fauconnier 1985, even Goodman's improbable counterfactual *If the match had been struck, it would not have been dry* (as opposed to: *If the match had been struck, it would have lit*) is appropriate in the right context. Similarly, the text example (7) is fine in a context where the key assumption is that we never have fun, no matter what.
4. E.g., structuralist, transformational, generative, gricean, searlean, montaguean, etc.
5. Reddy 1979; Lakoff and Johnson 1980; Turner 1986, 1991; Sweetser 1990 and forthcoming; Espenson 1991; and Goldberg 1994.
6. Langacker 1987, 1992; Lindner 1982; Brugman 1988; Goldberg 1992, 1994; Talmy 1991; Maldonado 1992; and Van Hoek 1991.

of analogical thought and its connection to seemingly more elementary linguistic processes,[7] frame semantics,[8] and recent advances in the study of conceptual development.[9]

This chapter examines several examples of counterfactuals in different grammatical constructions and analyzes the analogical mappings that come into play when such counterfactuals are understood via the construction of appropriate mental spaces. But first, a few words about analogy.

1. Analogy

The aspects of analogy that are relevant for present purposes have been studied insightfully in works such as Hofstadter (1985, 1995), Gentner (1983), Mitchell (1993), Gick and Holyoak (1983), and Turner (1991). They include:

• domain mapping from a source onto a target;
• extraction of an induced schema (or frame);
• extension, fluidity, and reanalysis.

1.1. Domain Mapping

Analogy maps partial structure of a source domain onto partial structure of a target domain. In a famous example studied by Gick and Holyoak, the medical problem of operating on a cancerous tumor using rays so as to avoid damaging healthy tissue is solved by analogy to the military problem of taking a fortress. The fortress maps onto the tumor, the general onto the surgeon, the columns of soldiers onto the rays. To take the fortress is to destroy the tumor; to send small convergent columns from different directions is to direct weak rays of different orientation that will converge to the same body area. The *source domain* of military strategy is mapped onto the *target domain* of medical surgery. And clearly, the mapping is restricted to a few counterparts and a very restricted amount of structure.

As Hofstadter emphasizes, the domains need not be different. For example, in a *Momma* comic strip, Momma's son, Francis, and his friend Jack are talking to Momma and showing her a credit card. Francis intends

---

7. Hofstadter 1985, 1995; Gentner 1983; Gick and Holyoak 1983; Orlich and Mandler 1992; Brown 1990; Turner 1991; and Sereno 1991a.
8. Fillmore 1982, 1985.
9. Bloom 1974, 1991; Mandler (forthcoming).

that his mother, Momma, will reason by analogy and draw appropriate conclusions; the analogy is meant to transfer the way in which Jack and his mother use the mother's credit card to Francis and Momma; it maps a social domain onto itself.

[The strip shows Francis and his friend Jack talking to Momma, Francis's mother, and showing her a credit card]

Jack: "This Visa card, Mrs. Hobbs? I use it and my mother pays the bills . . . so I never have to bother her for money!"

Francis: "Momma, can't I do that too?"

Momma: "It's fine with me."

[Then, last panel]

Momma: "Check with Jack's mother."

1.2. Induced Schemas

The structures mapped onto each other are mappable by virtue of being instances of a common, more abstract schema. The schema is a *frame* with *roles* that can be filled by elements of one or the other domain. The associated structures both fit the schema, and the schema specifies the mapping. In the Momma example, Francis intends the following schema to be extracted:[10] *son* uses *credit card* of *mother,* who pays *bills*.

There are (at least) four roles, *son, mother, credit card, bills,* interconnected by various relations. The relations fit into a rich inferential structure available through background knowledge. In the source situation, they are filled respectively by *Jack, Jack's mother, Jack's mother's card, Jack's bills.* In the target situation intended by Francis, they would be filled by *Francis, Momma, Momma's card, Francis's bills.*

1.3. Extension

For an induced schema to project structure from one domain to another, there has to be a partial mapping between the two domains. In the above example, the frame structure *son, mother, credit card, bills* allows Jack to be mapped to Francis, Victoria (Jack's mother) to be mapped to Momma, Visa card 112 to be mapped to Master Charge card 333, and so on.

10. I represent the schema in this ordinary language form for convenience. The psychological nature of frames is not crucial at this point.

The specific situation "Jack uses Visa 112 of Victoria to pay Jack's bills" is interpreted, via the corresponding roles, as an instance of the abstract schema:

son uses *credit card* of *mother,* who pays *bills,*

and that schema in turn gives a specific situation in the other domain, "Francis uses Master Charge 333 of Momma to pay Francis's bills."

Once the analogy has been triggered by a partial mapping, it is natural for further structure to get mapped, if this is a possibility. If Victoria, Jack's mother, pays the rent of Jack's sister, Annabelle, then perhaps Momma could pay Mary Lou's rent, and so on. A more extensive induced schema is produced. Besides being common in everyday reasoning, analogical extension is a crucial component of scientific innovation.[11]

Extension may also lead to the creation of new structure in the target domain. Suppose Mary Lou is still living at home. The extended mapping requires a counterpart for Annabelle's apartment—namely, an apartment for Mary Lou—not already present in the target domain. Finding such an apartment for Mary Lou creates the required new structure (under analogical pressure) and allows the analogical reasoning to proceed (i.e., Momma must pay the rent for the new apartment).

Or *extension* may lead to reinterpretation of old structure in the target. Perhaps Mary Lou owns a boat and pays for its upkeep. Annabelle's apartment can be mapped onto the boat, and the rent on the cost of the upkeep, triggering the inference that Momma should pay for the boat. Under that extension, the boat is now *thought of* as the equivalent for Mary Lou and Momma of the apartment for Annabelle and Victoria. New structure has been imposed on the target domain of Momma and her family. And this is possible through projection from the source domain of Victoria and her family.

1.4. Fluidity and Reanalysis

The case of the boat also illustrates the flexibility of analogy; reanalysis of the structural correspondences and extraction of new induced schemas are always possible. Deep analogy (Hofstadter 1985) is achieved by

---

11. A point often noted by analogy theorists. Having developed a conceptual analogy between parts of two domains (e.g., hydraulics and electricity), scientists will attempt to test and extend it for other parts of the domains. See Gentner 1983, Hofstadter 1985, Fauconnier and Turner 1994.

discovering and exploiting more abstract and less obvious schematic mappings.

There is never a "right" answer to the mapping problem, although given contexts will favor some mappings over others, as a function of the goals pursued and in keeping with general heuristics favoring structural relationships over simple attributes (Gentner 1983). Again, the *Momma* comic strip provides an illustration of this point. Guided by her own purpose in the conversation, Momma chooses to interpret her son's suggestion through a mapping that runs counter to our expectations and to Gentner's higher structure principle. In effect, Momma disregards the frame structure outlined above, and prefers to select the more superficial schema:

young man uses Victoria's Credit Card and Victoria pays *bills*

That schema involves only *two* roles, *young man* and *bills,* which are filled by Jack and Jack's bills in the source, and by Francis and Francis's bills in the target, yielding:

Francis uses Victoria's Credit Card and Victoria pays *Francis's bills.*

Victoria and her Credit Card are constants in this alternative schema and do not change when the roles receive different fillers.

Notice, in addition, that the anaphoric pronoun *that* in *Momma, can't I do that too?* has a very abstract antecedent, constructed by the analogical mapping. The antecedent will vary depending on which mapping (Francis's or Momma's) is constructed. This illustrates the more general point made by Dahl and Hellman (1995) that anaphoric links and antecedents are constructed dynamically in discourse. The case of co-reference with an explicitly introduced antecedent is just a special case.

The characteristics quickly outlined above are central to analogical reasoning. But they show up more generally in other kinds of *structure projection,* such as metaphor (whether entrenched or novel), metonymy, and pragmatic reference functions. The focus of this chapter is the presence of the very same characteristics in mental-space constructions, and specifically in those associated with counterfactual phenomena. Such phenomena, as it turns out, are based, just like analogy and other structure projections, on *domain mappings, induced schemas, extension,* and *reanalysis.*

2. Basic Observations: Counterfactuals and Frames

The analogical counterfactual phenomenon (Chapter 1, section 2.2.1) was pointed out in passing in Fauconnier (1990a) on the basis of examples like (8):

(8) *In France, Watergate wouldn't have done Nixon any harm.*

The point was that interpreting (8) as a comment on French politics and society is not a matter of examining the imaginary world in which Nixon was born or lived in France. Rather, it involves the extraction of a common frame for the American and French sociopolitical domains, and structure projection from the two domains to a third. The relevant triggering frame might include things like:

F ("Western Democracy frame"):
country has a **president** elected by **citizens**;
president is **head** of **political party** competing with others for leadership of **country;**
president's actions are constrained by **laws, public reaction,** ... ;
action brings harm to **president** if:
—it triggers negative **public reaction**
—it is unlawful and **president** is punished;
etc., etc.

[The bold-faced elements stand for roles; such a frame is typically part of an idealized cognitive model (ICM),[12] and it will bring in a huge amount of background knowledge structure in addition to the components crudely outlined here using English words and sentences.]

Sentence (8) builds up mental spaces in discourse in the following way. The initial space, B, is relative to the American political system at the time of Watergate. It contains frame F, with fillers (*values*) for the various roles:

president → Nixon
country → United States
citizens → Americans
law → no break-ins
punishment → impeachment
etc.

Space B, furthermore, contains information about Watergate itself,

12. Cf. Lakoff 1987.

which can be understood as a specific instance of a generic "break-in" frame:

("Break-in")
president secretly orders **break-in; break-in** fails and it is discovered that **president** was the instigator.

The role **president** is already filled by "Nixon"; the role **break-in** is filled by "Watergate." As before, the frame is actually much more complex than outlined here. The simplification, hopefully, will not alter the main characteristics of the process.

Finally, the initial space B contains information regarding the outcome of the specific events, which, again simplified, might include:

public reaction $\rightarrow$ outrage

punishment $\rightarrow$ impeachment

"Watergate does harm to Nixon" is understood as an instance of the subframe: **break-in** does harm to **president.**

Notice that all of this elaborate structure, which will be essential in order to make sense of sentence (8) when it comes along in some conversation or other form of discourse, is *not* in any way conveyed by sentence (8); it is purely background.

When sentence (8) is actually processed as part of a discourse, it starts with the space builder *in France*. This is going to bring in two new spaces. First, it brings in a space G (as in Gallic) corresponding to relevant partial background information about the *French political system*. This space will include a frame F′ sharing much of the structure of frame F in the base space: roles like **president, laws, country, public reaction,** and so on. The identical structure allows a mapping from space B to space G: shared roles and relations get mapped. The common structure of F and F′ is the schema that allows an initial mapping to be established. It corresponds to the basic *mother, son, credit card,* schema in the Momma example (*mother* of *son* has *credit card; son* has *bills* to pay).

After space G is set up, the sentence could proceed in the regular past tense, as in (9):

(9)   *In France, Watergate did not do Nixon any harm.*

A sentence like (9) would be saying something about the consequences of *Watergate* for *Nixon* in France. It would not use the extracted frames, it would not be analogical, and it would not be counterfactual.

Sentence (8), in contrast, because of the grammatical form *would not have done,* is counterfactual. And in terms of discourse construction, that translates into the introduction of a *third* mental space C (as in Counterfactual). Space C is counterfactually bound to G: it is setting up a (partially defined) situation in which, contrary to current knowledge, something "similar" to Watergate happens in France.

The process functions in the following way:

The space builder *in France* indicates that relevant background structure in C will be inherited from space G. This includes frame F'. The words *Watergate* and *Nixon,* however, *do not* point to elements of space G ("France"). They point to elements **w** and **n** of the base B ("United States"). As C is the space being structured,[13] the words *Watergate* and *Nixon* must ultimately identify elements of C.

Now, it is a fundamental property of mental spaces that such access is possible from one space to another when counterparts are mapped by connector functions. The general principle was introduced in Chapter 2, section 2.2:

Access Principle:[14] If connector Γ maps element **a** onto element **b**, element **b** can be identified by a linguistic expression pointing to **a**.

It follows that in the example at hand, *Watergate* and *Nixon* will identify counterparts of **w** and **n** (from space B) in the focus space C. How are such counterparts obtained? This is where the analogical mapping plays a key role: mental space C has inherited the "political" frame F' from G ("France"). And therefore it is (partially) mappable onto the base ("U.S."), which included frame F. Values ("role-fillers") are mapped onto values of the corresponding roles. This allows a straightforward mapping of **n** (Nixon) onto the value **n'** of the role **president** in space C. If there is a value for that role in G (e.g., Mitterrand), **n'** will also be the counterpart of that value in C (intuitively, Mitterrand in the counterfactual situation). If G is less specific (referring to French politics in general, independently of its particular instantiations), element **n'** has no counterpart in G. Informally speaking, **n'** is then a hypothetical French president involved in a Watergate-like situation.

---

13. C is the focus space at this point in discourse.
14. Also called the Identification (or I.D.) Principle.

Schematically:

Space B	Space C	Space G
Frame F	Frame F$'$	Frame F$'$
role: **president**	**president**	**president**
value: **n** (*Nixon*)	**n**$'$	"Mitterrand" or unspecified

Now, Watergate is not a value in the initial triggering frame F; but it is a value in the relevant additional frame BI (break-in). In order for Watergate to have a counterpart in C, this frame must be projected onto C, providing new structure:

Space B	Space C	Space G
Frame F	Frame F$'$	Frame F$'$
role: **president**	**president**	**president**
value: **n** (*Nixon*)	**n**$'$	"Mitterrand" or unspecified
Frame BI	Frame BI	
role: **break-in**	**break-in**	
value: **w** (*Watergate*)	**w**$'$	

The above cognitive construction is required before the content of sentence (8) can even start to be assessed. That content, relative to the counterfactual focus space C, is expressed by: *Watergate not do Nixon any harm. "In France"* and the grammatical aspect and tense (*would, have* + past) indicate what spaces are set up, with respect to which this content is to be evaluated. And by virtue of the Access Principle, this content reduces in space C to:

w$'$ "not harm" **n**$'$

That content is in opposition to the consequence of BI in space B, namely:

w "harm" **n**

At this point, space C is a "blend" of spaces B and G, with additional relations found in neither.[15] What is the use of C in the discourse? It does not give direct information about actual situations, and it does not represent existing frame configurations. However, besides being counterfactual, C is also *conditional*. The semantics linked to C include the general *matching* conditions on hypothetical spaces, discussed in the next chapter. The matching condition (an extended form of Modus

---

15. See Chapter 6 for a discussion of conceptual integration and blends, and a refinement of the analysis of counterfactuals in terms of blending.

Ponens) specifies in general that a space matching the defining structure of a conditional space fits it in all other respects.[16]

In the present case, the defining structure of C is frames F′ and BI, and its additional structure, introduced explicitly, is "**w′** not harm **n′**." It follows, therefore, from matching with C that a space with frames F′ and BI will also have the additional structure "**w′** not harm **n′**." This amounts to saying that frame F′, when combined with BI, yields different consequences from frame F combined with BI. Not surprisingly, then, the whole process ends up highlighting an important difference between the *existing* French and American political systems, based on their potential consequences, when confronted with similar contexts. It is, of course, notable that sentence (8) does not in itself tell us what these differences might be; it is up to the listener (and the speaker for that matter) to infer from background knowledge what existing differences might account for the different consequences. But conversation participants do not have to go through this extra inferencing in order to understand (8). Sentence (8) under this interpretation is falsifiable to the extent that a new situation might arise in which the French president *is* harmed by a secret break-in, yielding a factual basis for constructing a space that violates matching with C. It is also considered falsifiable in argumentative discourse by constructing such nonmatching spaces (counterfactually) by deductive, or analogical, reasoning from existing background knowledge.

One could counter (8), for instance, by saying:

(10)   *You're wrong. Look at all the harm the Greenpeace incident did to Mitterrand.*

The "Greenpeace incident" was not a break-in,[17] but it was widely believed to have been secretly and illegally approved by the French president.[18] A sentence like (10) widens frame BI, replacing the role **break-in** by a more general one. Real consequences become available to assess the "truth" of the counterfactual (8).

The theoretical implications of examples like (8) are far-reaching. The above analysis suggests that, as discourse unfolds and mental spaces are set up, the recovery of meaning fundamentally depends on the capacity

16. Technically, as developed in Chapter 5, the conditional consists of two spaces, the Foundation (the defining structure) and the Expansion.
17. A bomb planted by French agents exploded on the ship *Rainbow Warrior* and killed a photographer.
18. Encrevé (1988) provides an insightful analysis of the mental-space constructions and analogical connectors that were used by the daily newspaper *Liberation* in reporting the above-mentioned Greenpeace "incident."

to induce shared structures, map them from space to space, and extend the mappings so that additional structure is introduced and exported. This picture is quite different from the classical view that core literal truth-conditional meaning is first produced, and later altered, by more peripheral "pragmatic" operations.

Are the mechanisms operating in the interpretation of (8) representative of natural-language semantics? The remainder of this chapter will show that they are indeed pervasive and basic, and that they show up in various grammatical guises. Relevant examples will be discussed, using mental-space construction and linkage, as exemplified throughout this study and in Fauconnier (1985), Lakoff (1987), Sakahara (1990), Dinsmore (1991), and Marconi (1991), among others.

Such construction makes use of the assumptions and operating principles presented in Chapters 2 and 3:

- Background knowledge in the form of frames, idealized cognitive models, cultural models, folk theories, etc. is available.
- Local framing and (extensive) pragmatic information is available—for example, whether we are reading a story, watching a play, having an argument, reporting information, etc., where we are, who we're interacting with and why, etc.[19]
- Discourse construction starts in a *base* (also called "origin" or "current discourse"[20]) *space* from which a lattice of spaces related to each other will evolve.
- The spaces are used to build up cognitive structure and information relative to "objectively" very different kinds of things: time periods,[21] beliefs,[22] pictures, hypothetical or counterfactual situations, points of view,[23] quantifications, geographical locations,[24] cultural constructions.[25]
- At any point in the dynamic unfolding of space configurations, one space and one space only is "in focus"; various grammatical and pragmatic devices exist to switch focus.[26]
- The spaces are connected in two major ways: (1) by the ordering relation on the lattice: Each space is introduced relative to another (its "parent");

19. All this sounds perfectly trivial and commonsensical, and it is indeed for participants in the process, which makes it all the more frustrating when we fathom its formal complexity and scientific intractability.
20. Langacker 1992.
21. See Chapter 3, and Dinsmore 1991, Cutrer 1994, and Lansing 1992.
22. See Chapter 2.
23. See Chapter 3, Cutrer 1994, and Sanders and Redeker 1996.
24. See Van Hoek 1996.
25. See Rubba 1996.
26. See Chapter 3, Dinsmore 1991, Fauconnier 1991, Cutrer 1994, and Van Hoek 1996.

only when a space is in focus can it serve to launch a new child space; and
(2) by *connectors* that link elements across spaces, in accordance with the
Access Principle outlined above.

- Structure is transferred across spaces, in a variety of ways, which include:

    1. OPTIMIZATION: transfer by default from parent to child: Relevant struc-
    ture not explicitly contradicted is inherited within the child-space; this
    is a *downward* transfer in the space lattice; [example: *I wish Rosa's
    brother were kind* transfers to the "wish"-space properties satisfied in
    the Base—features of the individual independent of kindness, e.g., ap-
    pearance, being Rosa's brother, etc., even though such features are not
    themselves necessarily "wished for"].

    2. ACCESS: creation of counterparts via the Access Principle, as above with
    Watergate [example: Rosa and her brother have counterparts in the wish-
    space].

    3. PROJECTION of entire frames following the creation of a counterpart,
    again as in the *Watergate* instance, in a counterfactual space: the Break-
    in frame was projected along with the counterpart of element **w**; more
    generally, projection by extended mapping on the basis of initial partial
    mapping, as in metaphor, and analogy.

    4. MATCHING CONDITIONS for certain spaces (like hypotheticals), which
    allow additional structure to be transferred on the basis of partial fit [ex-
    ample: *If Maxine loves Max, then Max is happy* sets up a hypothetical
    space with the matching condition "LOVE (Maxine, Max)." The sat-
    isfaction of this condition in an appropriately related space will allow
    transfer of the remaining structure, "HAPPY (Max)]."[27]

    5. UPWARD FLOATING of presuppositions through the space lattice, until
    they meet themselves or their opposite. [This is the "projection problem"
    for presuppositions (Chapter 2, section 2.3.4). In (*a*) *Sue believes that
    George's son is bald*, the presupposition that George has a son floats up
    to the Base, but not in (*b*) *If George was a father, his son would be bald*,
    or in (*c*) *George has a son and Sue believes that George's son is bald*.
    (*b*) neither entails nor presupposes that George has a son; (*c*) entails but
    does not presuppose that George has a son.]

Optimization (downward) and Floating (upward) are both cases of
more general Spreading, a very powerful mechanism of structure building in natural language that allows large amounts of structure to be
transferred without explicit specification.

---

27. I call this Extended Modus Ponens because it is a generalization of the simple case: If space
H is connected to M, and H fits "P" and "Q," and M fits "P," then the additional structure "Q"
is mapped onto M via the appropriate connector. See Chapter 5 for a detailed exposition of
matching.

I now turn to cases that illustrate aspects of the relevant phenomena.

3. Spreading and Cancellation

From a *Drabble* comic strip comes this dialogue:

Dad (watching wrestling on TV): *When I was in my prime, I could've pinned Hulk Hogan in a matter of seconds!*
  Son (to mother): *Is that true, Mom?*
  Mom: *Probably.*
  Mom (next and last frame in the strip): *Of course, when your Dad was in his prime, Hulk Hogan was in kindergarten.*

Understanding this strip requires, among other things, that we understand the father to be saying that he used to be a top wrestler, and that we understand the mother's answer, superficially in agreement, as actually casting doubt on the "top wrestler" conclusion. Although the piece of discourse does not contain the typical grammatical markers for counterfactuals (*if, would*), it is understood through counterfactual mapping.[28]

Let's take a look at the space-building processes behind the dialogue. We use the notational conventions of Chapter 2. If a linguistic expression brings in a frame F, the notation Fxy will stand for "x and y fit frame F." So, for example, *Romeo is in love with Juliet* brings in a frame LOVE. If the expression is structuring some mental space M, and if *Romeo* and *Juliet* identify **a** and **b** in space M, then we will write: LOVE **a b** for the structure added to space M by the linguistic expression. A frame in this sense differs from a standard logical relation, in that (*a*) it may bring with it large amounts of background knowledge and inferences, (*b*) it will typically contain many roles (e.g., "rival," "parents," "meeting place," etc.).

PRIME **x** will abbreviate the content of **x** fitting the frame brought in by *to be in one's prime*. Such a frame typically carries inferences regarding an age range, a corresponding peak in health, physical abilities, and so on.

PIN **x y** will correspond to *pin someone in a matter of seconds,* with the corresponding implications (possibly by default) that "x" is stronger, a better wrestler, and so on, than "y."

---

28. "Could've" is not counterfactual in examples like *Hurry, get some help, he could've hurt himself.*

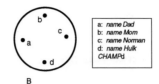

Figure 4.1.

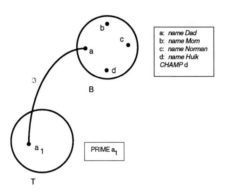

Figure 4.2.

CHAMP **x** will stand for being a talented wrestler, a champion, or as good as a champion.

The mental-space construction for the dialogue unfolds in the following way.

FIRST SPACE

Figure 4.1 shows the base B, for the comic strip, in which we have prior or inferred information about Mom, Dad, Norman, their son, and Hulk Hogan, the wrestling champion. Italics symbolize structure from background knowledge or default assumptions rather than explicitly introduced.

SECOND SPACE

When I was in my prime is a "past" space builder, which sets up a new space T relative to the base. There is a counterpart for "Dad" in this space, accessed through the pronoun *I*. This counterpart, a new element a_1 in T, is therefore linked to **a** by the Identity Connector $\Im$ as shown in Fig. 4.2.

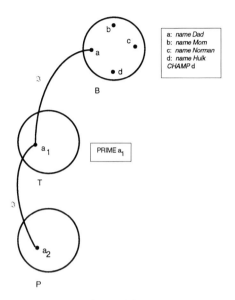

Figure 4.3.

The diagram reflects that a_1, but not its original counterpart **a**, satisfies the conditions associated with the PRIME frame.

THIRD SPACE

With *I could* …, the possibility modal *can* opens a new space of possibility P relative to the time space T. Grammatically, the modal is in the past tense (*could*); this is because the corresponding new space P has been opened "within" a past space.[29]

By virtue of the Access Principle, the pronoun *I*, subject of *could,* sets up a counterpart, a_2, for a_1 and **a** in the newly opened possibility space P, which is now in focus (see Fig. 4.3).

FOURTH SPACE

Another grammatical past now comes along in the form *have pinned.* The function of this second past tense is to mark not time but rather epistemic distance (Chapter 3, section 1.4); it is a *distal* in the sense of Langacker (1978), used here to set up a counterfactual space relative to

---

29. When a grammatical tense marks a property of some space in the space lattice, it also applies to structures in all spaces dominated by the initial one.

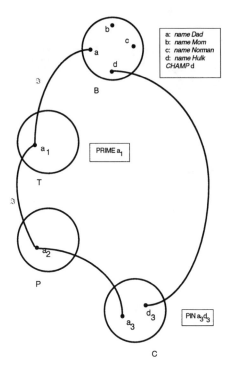

Figure 4.4.

P. Compare (11) and (12):

(11)   *In my youth, I could pin HH in seconds.*
(12)   *In my youth, I could have pinned HH in seconds.*

The present infinitive in (11) suggests that pinning HH actually did occur. The past in (12) seems to imply strongly that it did not.

After the distal past has applied, a fourth space C is set up, with counterparts for Dad and Hulk Hogan as shown in Fig. 4.4. The counterfactual space C includes a counterpart, d_3, of d in the base (*Hulk Hogan*). At this point in the construction, new structure is brought into C by Optimization: This is the default procedure that transfers structure associated with an element in one space to its counterpart in another. Optimization applies only if it does not lead to internal incompatibilities. In the present example, element d_3 inherits structure from its counterpart in the base, element d; this is the structure [*CHAMP* d_3].

Background knowledge of the form "he who pins down a champ is a champ" will add more implicit structure to space C, namely [*CHAMP* a_3]. At that point, the space configuration will be as in Fig. 4.5. In this

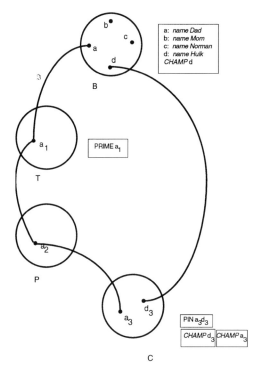

a: *name Dad*
b: *name Mom*
c: *name Norman*
d: *name Hulk*
CHAMP d

PRIME a_1

PIN $a_3 d_3$

CHAMP d_3 *CHAMP* a_3

Figure 4.5.

way, structure has been built in the lowest space, the counterfactual C. This implicit structure can then be propagated upward by Spreading. It will go up to the possibility space P, and then up again to the time space T, as in Fig. 4.6. Spreading is halted either logically (if a contradiction arises) or pragmatically, as in the present example: space T ("when I was in my prime") is explicitly set up as a focus of inference, and the inferred structure is understood to be time-dependent—being a champion wrestler is a state that is liable to change from youth to old age (according to our default cultural model). Hence the structure will not propagate beyond space T; we can infer that Dad was good in his prime, not that he still is. This aspect of Spreading is (unfortunately) not derivable from the space configurations alone; compare our example with the following:

(13)   *Don't make me mad. Remember that yesterday I could have knocked you out.*

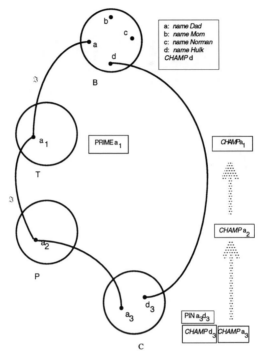

Figure 4.6.

One interpretation here is that if it was possible yesterday, it still is today. The relevant inference (e.g., "I am stronger than you") will (or at least can) spread all the way up.

The two similar examples with different spreading properties show that inference propagation takes the conceived real world into account. This stands in contrast to the structure propagation downward into the counterfactual—the championhood of Hulk Hogan projected from the base to a space linked to a remote time period.

To recapitulate: The important feature of this construction is the inheritance by default of the *CHAMP* structure for the counterparts of d in space C. This follows from Optimization, the default principle that transfers structure from the base to the new spaces T, P, and C. The structure obtained for C through this process, [*PIN* a_3 d_3][*CHAMP* d_3], warrants the crucial inference [*CHAMP* a_3], which in turn gets propagated back to space T. To put it less formally, counterparts for *Hulk Hogan* in the new spaces remain associated with the property of being a champion wrestler.

To beat Hogan is therefore also to be a champion wrestler. Space C is *counterfactual*, because the father will not and did not fight Hogan. This is why [*PIN* a_3d_3] cannot be transferred back to space T. The *CHAMP* structure, on the other hand, which holds for a_3 in C, does propagate to T (and it gets associated with a_1). As we might expect, then, the counterfactual construction yields the "real" past inference that the father used to be an outstanding wrestler.

The mother's contribution modifies the space construction. As pointed out by Y. Takubo, the mother's construction has counterparts d_1 and d_2 for d in the intermediate spaces T and P. The frame for d_1 linked to "_*be in kindergarten,*" and abbreviated as CHILD, is explicitly added to space T. The time difference between **B** and **T** that was left vague in the first construction is now inferred to be large by virtue of cultural knowledge about kindergarten and professional fighting. More importantly, the new explicit frame is incompatible with the implicit structure [*CHAMP*].[30] The explicit frame relations in T propagate to spaces P and C, effectively canceling the incompatible implicit structure [*CHAMP* d_3]. After the mother has spoken, the construction has shifted, as shown in Fig. 4.7.

What is striking about the example is the way in which the default strategies operate. Structure linked to element d in the base B (Hogan is strong, in his prime, a champion, etc.) propagates in spite of the fact that we "know" that going back in time to make Dad young should make Hogan much younger as well and remove his relevant properties (the realistic strategy implicitly adopted by the mother to justify her alternative construction). This highlights a general and distinctive property of counterfactuals: They are not intended to refer to realistic worlds; their power seems to lie instead in the inferences (produced through local space building) that they can project back to other spaces.

As we shall see in later examples, analogical mappings are at work here in different guises. In the *Drabble* example, for instance, the father's interpretation could be corroborated if space C matched a subspace of T— that is, if the father had indeed fought and beaten fighters "comparable" to Hogan: Space C works as a schema with minimal structure, and element d_3 is minimally specified; while the relevant *CHAMP* structure does get inherited by default, other properties of Hogan (the color of his hair, his phone number, the nationality of his mother, and such, if they happen to be specified in B) are weakly inheritable but do not count in assessing

---

30. Background cultural framing is necessary to obtain such incompatibilities.

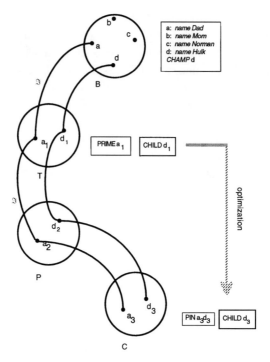

Figure 4.7.

the "truth-value" requested by the son. Even though the construction rests on what looks like a vivid and concrete image, the father fighting the Hulk, it allows a much more abstract schema to be extracted and used for reasoning, and for corroboration. This is also known to be an essential property of metaphorical mappings: A correspondence between vivid source and target domains allows abstract schemas to be extracted, transferred, or modified for the purpose of reasoning and organizing thought.

4. Fictitious Elements and Truth Conditions

4.1. The Naked Lie

The following dialogues are taken from a movie called *The Naked Lie*.

[Context: A prostitute has been found murdered; Webster (an unpleasant, self-centered character in the movie) shows no sympathy; Victoria disagrees with Webster.]

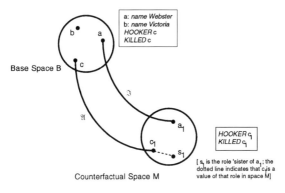

Figure 4.8.

Victoria: *What if it were your sister?*
Webster: *I don't have a sister, but if I did, she wouldn't be a hooker.*
[Later in the movie, Victoria talking to someone else]
Victoria: *You know that sister Webster doesn't have? Well, she doesn't know how lucky she is.*

The word *sister* brings in an important kinship frame that has interesting properties of its own, but I will simplify that aspect of the structure for present purposes, assuming only that a role s_i in some space containing a_i corresponds to the informal "sister of a_i." As with any other role, s_i may have a value or not in its space. If e is such a value, we shall use the notation $s_i \rightarrow e$ to indicate that e is a value of role s_i.

The first part of the example, the dialogue between Victoria and Webster, amounts to negotiated space building. Victoria develops a model which carries the intended inference that Webster should show sympathy, and this counterfactual model is analogical in interesting ways. Webster answers with a counterfactual model of his own, designed to foil the inference. Webster's model is also analogical.

Victoria's first contribution to the conversation sets up the space configuration in the obvious way, with the counterfactual space M as shown in Fig. 4.8. Notice that elements c and c_1 are linked by the *analogy* connector $\mathfrak{A}$, not by identity. That is, we interpret Victoria's question as saying, "What if, *instead* of happening to this girl, it had happened to your sister?" A very close construction differing only in types of connector would be produced by the sentence: *What if she were your sister?* The construal of this counterfactual would consist in keeping "the same" girl, but framing (!) her as Webster's sister.

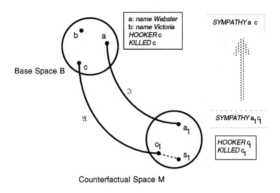

Figure 4.9.

Victoria's counterfactual "replaces" the real girl analogically by Webster's sister.[31]

Once the counterfactual has been set up, new inferences can be drawn (in space M) according to cultural models like "one should show sympathy if one's sister is killed," and then, as in the *Drabble* example, the new inferences will spread upward to counterparts in dominant spaces (see Fig. 4.9).

Although Victoria has not claimed that Webster had a sister, her use of the definite description *your sister* could be interpreted as presupposing that Webster has a sister. Element c_1 would then be linked by another connector (identity $\Im$) to an element c' in the base ("Webster's sister"), as in Fig. 4.10.

The diagram reflects that the base space B and the counterfactual space M are linked by two connectors: analogy $\mathfrak{A}$ and identity $\Im$. The roles for "Webster's sister" in the two spaces are s and s_1, linked by identity $\Im$. The values of these roles are c' and c_1, also linked by identity. The *analog* of c (the "hooker" in the base) is c_1 in the counterfactual space M. This is a case of double linkage, with one element in the counterfactual space linked to two elements in the base as shown in Fig. 4.11. As in many counterfactual constructions, we get a frame-blending effect: Element

---

31. Aspects of such counterfactuals are studied in Moser 1988, Fauconnier 1990b, and Lakoff 1996. The effect of the "it" construction used by Victoria is to build an analogue of the situation where one element (the hooker) gets replaced by another (the sister). Compare with:

    My cheap earrings were stolen. Lucky IT *wasn't my pearls.*
    *Lucky THEY *weren't my pearls.*

    In the other construction, *What if* SHE *were your sister?* a counterfactual is built with an identity connector. In the counterfactual, "she" is the same individual but has different properties, as in: My earrings were stolen. Lucky THEY weren't genuine.

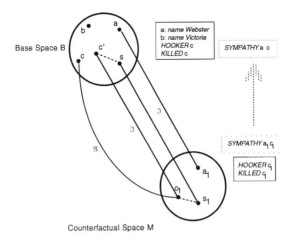

Figure 4.10.

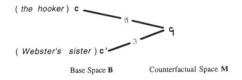

Figure 4.11.

c_1 fits into the two frames for c (the murdered hooker), and c′ (Webster's sister). And consequently, relevant properties of $\mathbf{c_1}$ can be derived, for instance, deserving sympathy from Webster; such properties are in turn transferred back to the base via the analogical connector $\mathfrak{A}$, and we get the inference intended by Victoria that Webster should show sympathy for the murdered woman.

The dialogue at this point can be thought of as a competition between the participants to build appropriate spaces and connections, and thereby obtain intended inferences within the discourse. Webster proceeds by attacking and destroying the construction just set up by Victoria from two directions. The first direction is a frontal attack. Webster says: *I don't have a sister.* This amounts to removing c′ from the base: the role s for *Webster's sister* no longer has a value. The transfer of the favorable "sister" frame to $\mathbf{c_1}$ is blocked, and so it looks as if the corresponding inferences are blocked, in particular, the need for Webster to show sympathy.

This is not entirely sufficient, however, because Victoria's counterfactual can be interpreted without the presupposition that Webster has

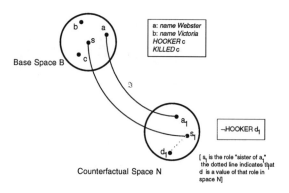

Figure 4.12.

a real sister. All that is needed is for c_1, the counterfactual element, to have the role s_1. In that alternative construction for Victoria's *"What if it were your sister?"* there is no value for the role Webster's sister (s) in the base, but in the counterfactual space the murdered woman is a value for the corresponding role (s_1). To undermine inferences stemming from this alternate construction, Webster's strategy is to block the property "hooker" that would attach to his sister. This is done at the role level: No sister of Webster's could ever be a hooker. In our formalism, this amounts to imposing the condition ¬ HOOKER (s_1) on the counterfactual space, which in turn prevents the counterpart c_1 from being linked to role s_1, because HOOKER(c_1) would contradict ¬ HOOKER(s_1).

In order to impose this condition, Webster has constructed a counterfactual space of his own, call it N, in which an imaginary sister makes an appearance, as shown in Fig. 4.12. The short exchange between Victoria and Webster (first part of dialogue) sets up three spaces B, M, and N. It links B to M and N by means of counterfactual connectors, and links B to M by means of an analogical connector. B is thus linked to M in two ways. This is already pretty fancy space construction for a perfectly ordinary piece of conversation.

The second part of the dialogue is less ordinary, in fact spectacular. *That sister Webster doesn't have* identifies an element in B, as confirmed by the use of the indicative in the next sentence. And this element d is presented as a counterpart in the base of d_1 in the counterfactual space N: Indeed, as the difference between B and N is whether Webster has a sister or not, any counterpart of d_1 in B will necessarily *not* be the sister of Webster. Hence d is associated with the property of not being Webster's sister, and as this is the only available property, the implicature will naturally be that this is the reason for her being lucky. This will transfer back in turn to N in negative form: d_1 "is unlucky" by virtue of "being Webster's sister." This will feed in turn into surface pragmatics to yield the desired negative evaluation of Webster. Even though d is an element set up in B, it has no reference; it is entirely fictitious and used only for the purpose of producing the implicature. Endpoints of scales can also be fictitious in this way, with elements nevertheless set up in the base.[32] The twist in the present case is Victoria's phrasing: *She doesn't know how lucky she is.* Although any referent chosen for d would normally know that she isn't Webster's sister and might also know that this is a good thing, she wouldn't know that she has escaped the fate of her counterpart in a world corresponding to space N.

The account just proposed has one drawback, however. It seems to introduce an element in the Base with a real referent (the lucky non-sister). This is not quite right if the Base corresponds to the speaker's reality. We shall see in Chapter 6 how to remedy this flaw by taking into account the fact that Victoria is also engaged in setting up a conceptual Blend.

Finally, there is a methodological point to be addressed in connection with examples like the above. Clearly they are facetious, and meant to be. Should our theory account for them? Do they show anything interesting? I take the following strong position in this respect, following Moser and Hofstadter (MS), Turner (1991): Errors, jokes, literary effects, atypical expressions use the same cognitive operations as everyday language, but in ways that actually highlight them and can make them more salient. As data, they have a status comparable to laboratory experiments in physics: They are things that may not be readily observable in ordinary circumstances, and which for that very reason shed light on underlying principles. Notice that no specialized linguistic devices are invoked to explain the Webster/Victoria example; rather, it is claimed that the very same construction principles operate here as in other counterfactuals and analogies. But it is a powerful property of this model that it allows for the production and understanding of "strange," "funny," "unusual" cases, and that it displays the respects in which they are untypical.

More generally, it has often been noted, and most forcefully by Cicourel (1996), that restricting one's attention to supposedly typical

---

32. *With this telescope, you can see <u>the most distant stars.</u>*
    Bart is incapable of solving <u>the simplest problem.</u>

    do not entail that there actually is a "simplest problem" or that some stars are "the most distant." The scalar endpoints are set up so as to trigger scalar quantification (... you can see any stars; Bart is incapable of solving any problem). See Fauconnier 1975.

isolated sentences with their default meanings is not really legitimate scientific idealization. It is liable to leave out the crucial elements upon which meaning construction actually depends. The rich data invoked in this study for analyzing mental-space phenomena corroborates this methodological point. The properties of simple defaults do not provide the principles needed for interpretation in general.

4.2. The Missing Tree

Ann Landers, the newspaper columnist, cites amusing formulations in insurance claims filed by people who wish to minimize their responsibility in an accident. Here is one of her examples:

Coming home, I drove into the wrong house and collided with a tree I don't have.

As in the previous case (*that sister Webster doesn't have*), we find a description here (of the tree) in terms of *nonexistence* (of its counterpart). As usual, devious (but not deviant) descriptions like this are possible because of the Access Principle, which allows connecting paths across spaces. In Fig. 4.13, the counterfactuality and the analogy are triggered by the word *wrong*. Two domains are set up, one for the right house, one for the wrong one:

space R

h	role for a location ("house")
h → b	value for that role in space R
a	("speaker")
t	role for a tree in location h
t → ∅	(no value for the role—i.e., no actual tree in that location)
a "drives safely into" h	

Space W

h′
h′ → b′
a′
t′
t′ → c′
a′ "collides with" b′

A good description of t in R is "*tree I don't have*," as in:

Our houses are similar, except that I don't have that tree in the back.
Your book has a chapter in it that mine doesn't have. [*not have* can express the absence of value for a role]

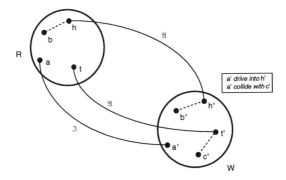

Figure 4.13.

The connecting path across spaces and from role to value will link t to its counterpart t' and then to the value b'. In this way b' will be identified (by the description for t).

The counterfactual here is space R (corresponding to what should have happened) as opposed to what did (space W). Relevant to the present discussion is the nature of the connector linking the two spaces: It is overtly analogical—the two houses and tree locations are in no way presented or conceived as identical, just analogous. A fascinating pragmatic feature that we won't go into here is the explanatory value of this construal for the insurance report.[33]

5. Mixing Frames and Blending Spaces

Another dimension of the phenomena studied in this chapter is explored in Fauconnier and Turner (1994) and in Chapter 6 of this book: the extent to which spaces that are connected analogically can give rise to new "blended" spaces in which cognitive work is accomplished. It is claimed that conceptual blending is a general instrument of cognition running over many linguistic and nonlinguistic cognitive phenomena, such as

---

33. A reviewer pointed out the interesting use of the definite article in "the wrong house" and noted the similarity to "I dialed the wrong number." The definite signals the role, which is unique in the prototypical frame of "wrong vs. right" number or house—you only dial *one* number, even though objectively the set of wrong numbers or wrong houses is very large. Here is a striking example of this use:

ERROR REPORTED IN BREAST CANCER STUDY:

... The researchers had said heredity appears to account for about 2.5% of total breast cancer cases, but corrected that to 6%. ... "We took the wrong number and multiplied it by the wrong number," said Dr. Graham A. Colditz, a coauthor of the study. ... [newspaper clipping, *Los Angeles Times*]

categorization, inference, grammatical constructions and functional assemblies, action frames, analogy, metaphor, and narrative. As noted above, space C in the Watergate/Nixon example is a blended space. So are spaces C in the Hulk Hogan case and space M in the Naked Lie case.

Blending is usually invisible to consciousness, but there are highly noticeable cases in cartoons and metaphors. Interesting discussion of such cases can be found, in particular, in Talmy (1978), Hofstadter et al. (1989), and Moser and Hofstadter (MS). Goffman (1974) displays striking cases of frame mixing, viewed from a sociological standpoint.

The following attested example from everyday conversation in French shows the complexity of blended analogical counterfactual spaces:

> Brigitte: *Muriel pourrait facilement être la mère de son petit frère.* [Muriel could easily be the mother of her little brother.]
> Catherine: *Oh oui, moi à cet âge, je serais la mère de son petit frère.* [Oh yes, me at that age, I would be the mother of her little brother.][34]

Brigitte in effect sets up a counterfactual space, with two elements, "mother" and "son," mapped onto "sister" Muriel and her "brother" in space B. Age is the only relevant property and is maintained across spaces. Notice that identification is in terms of roles *mère* and *frère*, each one from a different space.

Catherine sets up a time space for when she was Muriel's age. In that space, the element c′ that refers to Catherine actually has the role "mother" with a corresponding child the same age as Muriel's brother. So it can get mapped onto a counterfactual in which the child becomes a counterpart of Muriel's brother, and c′'s counterpart inherits the "mother" property from c′. In plain English, Catherine is saying (in French) that when she was Muriel's age, she had a child the same age as Muriel's brother. And this corroborates Brigitte's statement, by giving real evidence for the possibility of being Muriel's age and having a child the same age as her brother.

Notice in particular how Catherine is *not* identifying with the mother of Muriel's brother, whose age is bound to be much older, as she is also Muriel's mother.

Because the point of this dialogue happens to be relative ages of siblings, on the one hand, and parent and child, on the other, other properties are only weakly transferred: the mappings take place on the basis of age analogy and motherhood only (see Fig. 4.14).

---

34. The conditional *serais,* like its English counterpart *would be,* would be judged ungrammatical by natives. Nevertheless, it was produced in context, because the "grammatical" *aurais été* (would have been) carries extra (unwanted) referential implications.

S<small>PACE BUILDING</small> (simplified by leaving out all the roles):[35]

    (Base)
    B: a   name *Muriel,* age 24
       b   brother of a, age 2
       c   name *Catherine,* age 46
    (Counterfactual possibility)
    M: a′   mother of b′, age 24
       b′   son of a′, age 2
    (Past)
    T: c′   name *Catherine,* age 24, mother of d
       d   child of c′, age 2
    (Counterfactual relative to T)
    Q: c″   age 24, mother of b″
       b″   child of c″, age 2

C<small>ONNECTORS</small>: Identity and Analogy link b to b′; Identity links c, c′, c″, on the one hand, and b, b″, on the other.

Crucially, Analogy links d to b″, and to b′. Analogy also links a′ to c″ (this happens because of the corresponding motherhood and age structures in spaces M, T, Q). Linguistic evidence for the links is tied to the application of the Access Principle along the connecting paths: b″

---

35. With the roles:

    B: σ sister of β
      β brother of σ
      $\sigma \to \mathbf{a}$
      $\beta \to \mathbf{b}$
    M: μ mother of γ
      γ child of μ
      $\mu \to \mathbf{a'}$
      $\gamma \to \mathbf{b'}$
    T: $\mu \to \mathbf{c'}$
      $\gamma \to \mathbf{d}$
    Q: $\mu \to \mathbf{c''}$
      $\gamma \to \mathbf{b''}$

This allows a more careful syntactic analysis: *la mère de son petit frère* is role $\langle \mu, \mathbf{b'} \rangle$ (mother of **b′**), with **b′** identified via the role $\langle \beta, \mathbf{a} \rangle$ (brother of Muriel), and its value **b** in the base. The first sentence (Brigitte's statement) sets up M (*pourrait*), and identifies **a′** as the value of role $\langle \mu, \mathbf{b'} \rangle$:

Muriel être la mère de son petit frère
$$\mathbf{a'} \leftarrow \langle \mu, \mathbf{b'} \rangle$$

And so on. We can link the grammar elegantly to the space building. Furthermore, the role structure brings out clearly the basis for the analogical mapping. In the structures for T and Q above, we see **d** and **b″** occupying the same structural positions.

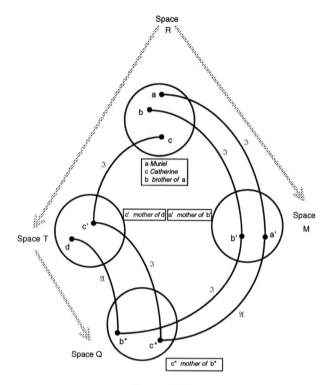

Figure 4.14.

in Q is identified by the description *son petit frère* (her little brother), which applies to b in the base space B.

It is interesting to note that while the point of the dialogue is to comment on the age difference between brother and sister, Catherine also makes the point that she was a young mother compared perhaps to the next generation, exemplified by Brigitte and Muriel who are twenty-four but have no children and are single. Believe it or not, in the real-life situation where this dialogue occurred, Brigitte was the daughter of Catherine (i.e., the analogical counterpart of Muriel's brother)!

6. Conclusion...

... insightfully provided by Anna Bosch, who noted the following country-music lyrics:

If you'd only put yourself in my shoes, you'd have some sympathy
And if I could put myself in your shoes, I'd walk right back to me.

Chapter 5
Matching

One way to think of space building, as determined by linguistic and non-linguistic features of the ongoing discourse and discourse setting, is to view the configurations as imposing constraints on available interpretations and subsequent configurations.[1] There is an array of operators, such as *if, when, where, or, whenever, supposing that,* which are understood to open spaces and impose **matching** conditions on related spaces.

1. Matching and Structure Projection

We shall say quite generally that space M with structure μ matches space N with structure ν via connector C, if structure μ can be mapped by connector C onto a substructure of ν. Two distinct questions arise: (1) the specification of the matching conditions; (2) what spaces are subject to the matching constraints, and what connectors are involved?

We shall first consider (1). Matching operators open two new spaces, a *foundation* space and an *expansion* space. The expansion is subordinate to the foundation (see Fig. 5.1).

Let me illustrate the concept with the operator *if*. At some stage in the discourse construction, an expression of the form

If A, then B

is introduced, relative to a space M in focus. A foundation space F subordinate to M is constructed by applying the instructions of language expression *A*. An expansion space E subordinate to F is constructed by applying the instructions of *B* to a copy of F. Formally, let μ be the structure of M at the point of the discourse where the matching operator comes in; let ϕ be the structure derived by applying language expression *A*, and let ε be the structure derived by applying expression *B*.

The following space configuration is set up (see Fig. 5.2).

1. This idea is explored in Fauconnier 1990b.

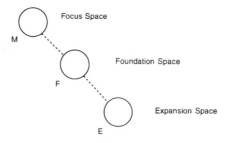

Figure 5.1.

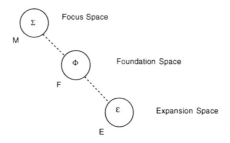

Figure 5.2.

The configuration {F, E} can now be used to build inferences in some[2] target space S by applying the matching instructions:

MATCHING: (*a*) check that the *foundation* matches the *target* (F matches S); (*b*) project the structure of the *expansion* onto the target (ε of E onto S).

To see how this works, consider some examples:

(1)   *If Olga is in the shower, Paul is in the kitchen.*

Expression (1) occurs at some stage of the discourse, relative to space M. Space M at that point has some structure [a, b, . . .] {Σ}, with a and b the elements corresponding to "Paul" and "Olga." We get the following configuration after (1) comes into the discourse, as shown in Fig. 5.3.

Assume that further dialogue elaborates M, for example:

(2)   *It's hot. There's noise in the street. Paul is unhappy. Olga is taking a shower.*

---

2. The distinct question of which spaces are affected will be examined presently.

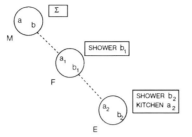

Figure 5.3.

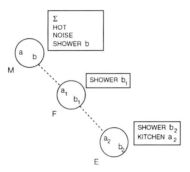

Figure 5.4.

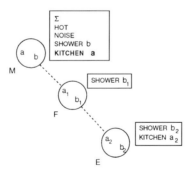

Figure 5.5.

The resulting configuration is Fig. 5.4. In this new configuration, the foundation space F <u>matches</u> space M: because b_1 is a counterpart of b, the structure of F is mappable onto a substructure of space M. It follows through matching that the structure of the expansion space E will be projected onto M, yielding (Fig. 5.5).

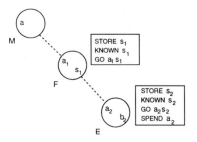

Figure 5.6.

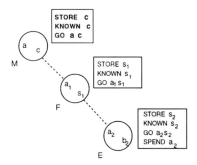

Figure 5.7.

In other words, we have the correct inference relative to M that Paul is in the kitchen.

When a new element is introduced directly into a foundation space, it is always a *role*. Consider a piece of discourse like the following:

(3)   *If Paul goes to a well-known store, he will spend money.*
(4)   *Paul went to Woolworth.*

When (3) occurs, the indefinite *a well-known store* sets up a role s_1 in the foundation space F (see Fig. 5.6).

When expression (4) comes in, an element c corresponding to "Woolworth" is set up in M. Background knowledge (Woolworth is a well-known store) lets in structure relative to c as shown in Fig. 5.7.

With s_1 as a role and c as a value, we now find that the foundation F can be mapped onto space M:

• Map elements i_1 onto their counterparts i, via connector I, e.g., a_1 to a. [Connector I is a connector linking spaces in the standard sense; there could be more than one available in a given context.]

Figure 5.8.

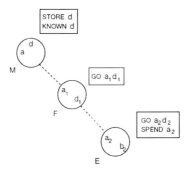

Figure 5.9.

- Map roles r_1 onto elements via the role-value connector V. In the example considered, we map s_1 onto c.

The foundation F will match the target M if all conditions satisfied by a role in F are satisfied for the value of that role in M. In our example we have matching because c fits the frame defined by s_1: It satisfies the conditions {STORE_}, {KNOWN_ }, {GO a_}.

Because the foundation fits the target, the expansion space can be projected onto M as in shown in Fig. 5.8.

Conceptually, a matching structure (foundation + expansion) allows a sort of generalized Modus Ponens to operate on spaces: By matching the foundation to the target, the expansion is exported.

As in other cases of space building, we have significant underspecification here. For example, in (3) the indefinite *a well-known store* sets up a new element in one of the available spaces (M or F), but it is not specified grammatically which one. In the above analysis, the new element came into F. If we chose the interpretation where it comes into M, we would have Fig. 5.9.

This, of course, is the interpretation commonly called specific, or outer scope. In this case, the inference that Paul will spend money holds only for a particular well-known store, and we are not told explicitly

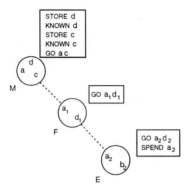

Figure 5.10.

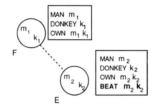

Figure 5.11.

which one. The inference drawn from Paul's going to Woolworth is not valid under this interpretation; the structure set up by (4) would be as shown in Fig. 5.10.

In this case, there won't be a match, because {GO a_1d_1} in F does not have a counterpart in M.

The other underspecified aspect of *matching* is the range of applicability of the matching structure. Consider the notorious "donkey" sentences:[3]

(5)   *If a man owns a donkey, he beats it.*

It sets up the matching structure of Fig. 5.11.

If space M is structured by the information that Buridan owns the donkey Hansel, the foundation F will match it as in Fig. 5.12. The projection of E onto M yields Fig. 5.13. A useful way to think about the process is to see the foundation space as setting up a frame of "donkey

3. Geach 1962.

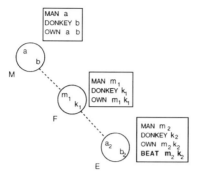

Figure 5.12.

Figure 5.13.

owners," and the expansion as adding properties to the frame: "donkey owners who beat their donkeys." When the foundation can match the target, then additional structure from the expansion can be added to the target.

So far the system runs fairly smoothly: Expression (5) can produce the correct inference that Buridan beats Hansel. However, this does not yet take into account that the conditional can apply to different kinds of domains. Expression (5) could be meant to apply generally: *All donkey owners beat their donkeys; they always have and they always will;* less generally: *In this part of the land, during some contextually specified time period, in some relevant group of people, donkey owners beat their donkeys* (e.g., "This is a farm that's run very harshly; if a man has a donkey he beats it."); to a fictional domain, with a general interpretation:

(6)   *In that movie, if a man owns a donkey, he beats it.*

Expressions like (5) can also apply in a more "punctual" sense to a present state of affairs: We're not sure about what's going on, but we conclude that if there is currently a donkey owner in our midst, he beats his donkey. This interpretation will not have even restricted universal consequences; it will not entail that donkey beating is common, or will occur in the future, and so on.

It is important, then, when using matching configurations to export structure, to know what domain types they apply to, even though that is seldom fully specified grammatically. The problem is clearly one of "relevance." In the farm example, only men and donkeys on that particular farm are considered; in the discourse, the partitioning is achieved by having a space set up for the farm domain. Similarly, a space is set up to talk about a particular movie or a particular time period, and application of *matching* is limited to that space.

More generally, within a discourse, domains and domain types (e.g., movies, times, countries, beliefs, . . .) are singled out, and spaces will be of various domain types. The range of application of a matching configuration will typically be understood pragmatically to be limited to spaces associated with a certain domain or domain type. Likely candidates are always:

- the base;
- the space currently in focus;
- a generic space for a certain domain type, often associated with the space currently in focus.

The base choice corresponds to the most universal interpretations (*All owners beat their donkeys always everywhere, or at least in a wide range of domains*); the focus choice corresponds to the more punctual readings (*If there is an owner, he beats his donkey*); the generic choice corresponds to a limited range of domains considered (*In movies like this, if a man owns a donkey, he beats it*).

I will assume in what follows that a combination of pragmatic and grammatical factors makes the appropriate domain type accessible. Clearly, however, this is at present an unsolved (although unavoidable) problem. In context, we have no trouble telling what the domain type is. How we do it is far from understood.

2. Domain Operators

Important work in semantics done by Carlson (1979), Farkas and Sugioka (1983), and Declerck (1988) has dealt with sentences like

(7) *Bears are intelligent when they have blue eyes.*

We think of *when* as prototypically temporal, but in expressions like (7), it clearly is not. Rather, the superficial effect of using *when* in (7) is to partition the set of bears, ascribing the predication in the main clause (intelligent) only to a subset of bears (those with blue eyes).

Declerck notes that *when*-clauses of this type are not equivalent to relative clauses, and in fact that there may be no overt anaphoric relation specified between the *when*-clause and the noun phrase corresponding to the partitioned set:

(8)   *When the husband or wife was dead, one relative rather than several tended to assume responsibility for the survivor. [from Edgren 1971]*

(9)   *Restaurants are bad places to eat when the head waiter is greedy. [from Carlson 1979]*

Declerck, correctly I think, takes the interpretation of *when* to be something like "in cases such that," restricting the cases in which the main clause is to be considered true. This characterization, however, is intuitive and does not, per se, yield the desired truth conditions for sentences like (7), (8), and (9). In fact, the actual relevant inferences of this type of sentence are quite diverse. In addition to (7), (8), and (9), consider the following:

(10)   *Sean Connery is invincible when he's James Bond.*

(11)   *Sean Connery is an excellent actor when he's James Bond.*

(12)   *When the heir to the throne is not very intelligent, he is likely to have difficulties with the army. [Declerck]*

(13)   *When the heir to the throne is chosen by Parliament, it is hard for him to govern.*

(14)   *When rhinoceri have two horns, they're cute.*

(15)   *When rhinoceri are widespread, they do a lot of damage to the forest.*

In (7) and (9) we have a partition on the bears and the restaurants. In (8) there is no partition of the relatives, but rather, presumably, of the "families." In (10) and (11) it is not Sean Connery who gets "partitioned," but rather the movies in which he plays. (12) and (13) distinguish different kinds of heirs, but (13) may also be taken as a statement about constitutions, thus partitioning countries or regimes. (14) is like (7): It singles out a special subset of rhinoceri. But (15) does not: It singles out regions with an abundance of rhinoceri.

The important thing to stress here is that the analysis of *when* as defining cases does not help to account for this wide array of possible interpretations, simply because there is no adequate truth-functional account of "X in cases such that Y." This situation is similar, from a theoretical point of view, to the case of counterfactuals mentioned in section 4.2, above (*In France, Watergate wouldn't have done Nixon any harm*): A single structure allows diverse interpretations that do not share a common truth-conditional core. But just like the counterfactuals in question, *when*-constructions can be treated uniformly once the intermediate cognitive level C is taken into account: Their common feature is to set up a connected domain with a general matching condition and underspecified pragmatic parameters. These operations take place at level C.

We use the properties of *matching* outlined in the previous section.

MATCHING OPERATOR *WHEN*

English grammatical construction: *When A, C*.

SPACE BUILDING: *When* is a matching operator; relative to the current Focus Space M, it sets up a Foundation Space F, internally structured by *A*, and an Expansion Space E, internally structured by *C*.

DOMAIN TYPE: A domain type D is specified pragmatically in the context of discourse.

PRESUPPOSITION OF EXISTENCE: Relative to the current Focus Space M, it is presupposed that there are domains of type D which fit the matching structure defined by F.

MATCHING CONDITION: Spaces of domain type D, which are matched by the Foundation, can be expanded by projection of the Expansion.

To see how this works, consider some relevant examples.

2.1. The Heir to the Throne

(16)   *When the heir to the throne is not very intelligent, he has trouble with the army.*

Under one interpretation, the roles "heir to the throne" and "army" call up the domain type "kingdom." *When* sets up a foundation space F with roles h and a, relative to whatever space M is in focus, and an expansion space E relative to F. ℑ is an identity connector between spaces (solid arcs on Fig. 5.14).

Suppose now that a particular kingdom is in question, relative to whatever domain the Focus space M corresponds to (speaker's real-

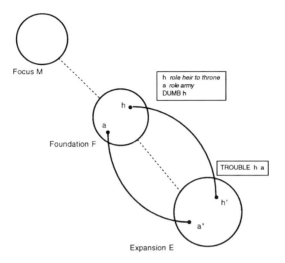

Figure 5.14.

ity, someone's beliefs, past time, fiction, etc.). Let us call the kingdom Atlantia, its army Tlan, and the heir to the throne Arthur. In the *discourse,* a corresponding mental space K, for the specific kingdom Atlantia, will be opened, subordinate to M. Because K is of the same domain type as F there will be counterparts h″ and a″ for the roles h and a. And these counterpart roles will have values i and j. Assume further that Arthur is indeed not very intelligent. The space configuration has been expanded to Fig. 5.15.

This configuration satisfies all the conditions for *expansion by matching:* mental-space K is of the same domain type as Foundation (mental) space F, and F <u>matches</u> K, via the (composite) connector going from roles in F to values in K: The structure of F [DUMB h] maps on the substructure of K, [DUMB i]. It follows that the structure of the Expansion space E can be <u>projected</u> into Focus space K. This means projecting [TROUBLE h′ a′] onto [TROUBLE i j] (see Fig. 5.16).

Notice that if we call $\mathfrak{B}$ the connector from roles to values, matching and expansion are carried out via the composite connector $\mathfrak{B} \circ \mathfrak{I}$ from roles in E to values in K. We assume that $\overline{\mathfrak{I} \circ \mathfrak{I}} = \mathfrak{I}$.

$$i = \mathfrak{B}(h'')$$
$$h'' = \mathfrak{I}(h)$$
$$h = \mathfrak{I}(h')$$
$$i = \mathfrak{B}(\mathfrak{I}(\mathfrak{I}(h'))) = \mathfrak{B}(\mathfrak{I}(h')) = \mathfrak{B} \circ \mathfrak{I}(h')$$

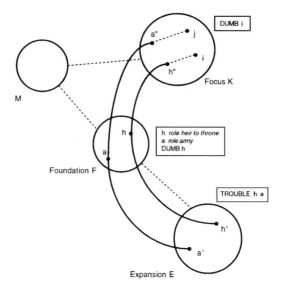

Figure 5.15.

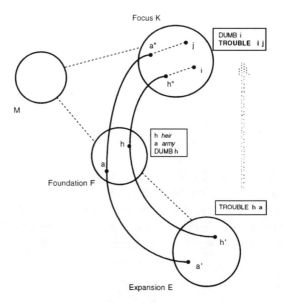

Figure 5.16.

and similarly

$$j = \mathfrak{B} \circ \mathfrak{I}(a') \tag{5.1}$$

Matching, via the composite connector, produces the desired inference in this context that Arthur will have trouble with Tlan, the army of Atlantia.

Now, let us *vary* the interpretation parameters to see how different understandings could be obtained for example (16). Suppose that in Atlantia it is in general the case that the heir to the throne is not very intelligent. Then [DUMB h'] is satisfied in space K. It follows that this space K <u>matches</u> space F (the foundation) *via* connector $\mathfrak{I}$. Structure from E (the expansion) can therefore be projected via connector $\mathfrak{I}$. Structure [TROUBLE h' a'] projects as: [TROUBLE h" a"].

Because h" and a" are roles, this structure expands the political frame of Atlantia: It represents the correct inference that, in Atlantia, the heir to the throne in general has trouble with the army.

Change the *domain type* from "kingdoms" to "times." F and K are now time spaces. With the mapping $\mathfrak{B} \circ \mathfrak{I}$ from roles to values, and the assumption that people's intelligence can change across time, we get the inference that if this is a time ("K") when Arthur is not very intelligent, then he will have trouble with Tlan. If the mapping is $\mathfrak{I}$, from h' to h", we get the more general inference that "at times when the heir to the throne of Atlantia is not very intelligent, that heir will have trouble with Atlantia's army." Other domain types (e.g., fairy tales, movies, newspaper reporters' beliefs) would yield logically different but cognitively similar inferences.

Matching accounts in a powerful way for the rich inferential potential of a single grammatical structure. Pragmatic parameters can vary without altering the grammatical and cognitive construction. Further examples will help to illustrate the generality of matching.

2.2. Widespread Rhinoceri

Compare the following three examples:

(17)   *When rhinos have blue eyes, they're cute.*
(18)   *When rhinos love each other, they're happy.*
(19)   *When rhinos are widespread, they have fun.*

Examples like these fit into different surface inference patterns:

When rhinos have blue eyes, they're cute.
Alix is a rhino.
Alix has blue eyes.

Therefore Alix is cute.

but not:

When rhinos love each other, they're happy.
Alix is a rhino.
*Alix loves each other.

Therefore, Alix is happy.

and not:

When rhinos are widespread, they have fun.
Alix is a rhino.
*Alix is widespread.

Therefore, Alix has fun.

(31) allows the pattern:

When rhinos love each other, they're happy.
Alix and Aline are rhinos.
Alix and Aline love each other.

Therefore, Alix and Aline are happy.

But (32) doesn't:

When rhinos are widespread, they have fun.
Alix and Aline are rhinos.
*Alix and Aline are widespread.

Therefore, Alix and Aline have fun.

Nor do we have patterns like:

When rhinos are healthy, they're widespread.
Alix is a rhino.
Alix is healthy.

*Therefore Alix is widespread.

In mental-space constructions for such examples, *rhinos* identifies a role *r* with individual elements or (plural) sets as its possible values. For

(17) the construction might include:

$$\begin{aligned}
\textit{Foundation Space}: &\ [\text{BLUE EYES r}][\text{RHINO r}] \\
\textit{Expansion Space}: &\ [\text{HAPPY r}'] \\
\textit{Focus Space}: &\ [\text{BLUE EYES a}][\text{r} = \mathfrak{B}(\text{r}'')]
\end{aligned}$$

Expansion via $\mathfrak{B} \circ \mathfrak{I}$ will straightforwardly project structure [HAPPY a] into the Focus Space.

In the case of (31), the predicate *love each other* imposes a set value for role r and its counterparts. The language expression *Alix* and *Aline* identifies such a value, c. The matching condition [LOVE c] will allow projection of [HAPPY c] from the Expansion (where it has the form [HAPPY r′]) into the Focus. Because the property HAPPY is also distributive (as opposed to LOVE), the structures [HAPPY a] and [HAPPY b] will also be added.

In the case of (32), a plausible *domain type* might be "countries." A valid inference pattern is:

When rhinos are widespread, they have fun.
In Kenya, rhinos are widespread.
Alix is a rhino in Kenya.

Therefore, Alix has fun.

In Kenya opens up a mental space of the appropriate domain type (countries). It matches the Foundation: [WIDESPREAD r″]. This allows Expansion Projection: [FUN r″]; and by distributivity of FUN: [FUN a].

2.3. Spies and Beautiful Women

(20) *When he's a spy, beautiful women fall in love with Sean Connery.*

Background knowledge about Connery and acting allows "movies" to be chosen as the domain type for this example. The drama connector $\mathfrak{D}$ linking actors and characters becomes available.

Suppose the particular movie *From Russia with Love* comes into the conversation, bringing in space M. In the movie, Sean Connery plays the part of spy James Bond. The Base element a, corresponding to the actor Connery, is mapped onto role r in the Foundation Space. The Matching Structure in F is: [SPY r]. Element a, in the Base, is mapped onto a′ (with role r″) in the movie space M. Since r″ fits the frame SPY, it connects to r in the Foundation, and r′ in the Expansion. The Expansion, which under this interpretation is also of the domain type "movie," will project the structure [LOVE b r′] to space M.

Element *b* ("beautiful women") has a counterpart b″, with value *b*, in M, and we get: [LOVE b a′]. In the <u>movie</u> *From Russia with Love,* one or more beautiful women (characters) fall in love with James Bond.

There are, of course, several other ways to connect and match the spaces for a discourse containing this example. As usual, the grammar *underspecifies* the construction. Obvious interpretations include the actor being a real spy at certain times, and having either real women or women in his movies fall in love with him. Or the actor playing the spy, and having real women love him in real life as a result. Or having real women fall in love with the character he plays (a *Purple Rose of Cairo* type of interpretation). And so on.

3. Meta-metaphorical Conditionals

The outline of matching in section 1 amounted to a sort of extended Modus Ponens. When the antecedent condition (Foundation Space) is satisfied, the consequent is also satisfied (Expansion Space). Section 2 showed that a more sophisticated version of matching actually operates, with the possibility of a variety of connectors, and composite functions. A very nice study by Eve Sweetser (forthcoming) shows another dimension of the matching process. She presents the following kind of data:

If the Ile de la Cité is the heart of Paris, then the Seine is its aorta.
If Scarlett O'Hara is a red rose, then Melanie Wilkes is a violet.

Clearly, such conditionals are not entailments at the level of content. The issue is not whether Scarlett and Melanie are actually flowers. Rather, the Foundation Space in these examples sets up a metaphorical mapping between two domains. The Expansion Space elaborates the mapping. Matching in these cases amounts to saying that, if one part of the metaphorical mapping is appropriate, then the other part must be too. Accordingly, the construction cannot juxtapose just any two metaphors:

If life is a candle flame, then people are moths burned on that flame.
*If life is a candle flame, then people are elephants.

However, Sweetser notes that two distinct metaphors can be so linked if they are being constructed according to the same principles:

If the Ile de la Cité is the heart of Paris, then Columbia is the brain of New York.

It turns out that the pattern completion from the Foundation to the Expansion in such cases is justified by general principles of reasoning as applied to metaphor. So, *If Paris is a body, the Ile de la Cité is its heart* reflects that if the whole-to-whole mapping is in place, the corresponding part-to-part mapping is also in place. *Scarlett is a rose* invokes a higher-level conventional metaphor that WOMEN ARE FLOWERS, in which Melanie also has a counterpart. *If the Ile de la Cité is the heart of Paris* contains Turner's (1991) XYZ construction: The Ile de la Cité is explicitly mapped to a heart; Paris must be mapped to a body; and the Seine is assumed to have a counterpart *within* this mapping. But the Columbia example allows access to an even higher superordinate mapping. From the XYZ metaphor created in the Foundation Space, "PARIS IS A HUMAN BODY," we can invoke (in the Foundation), the higher-level mapping "LARGE CITIES ARE HUMAN BODIES." In a mental space satisfying this matching condition, a specific city, New York, is then also a human body, and a part of it, Columbia, has a biological counterpart.

Citing, in addition to the meta-metaphors, cases like the analogical counterfactuals of Chapter 4, Sweetser concludes that conditionals of this type are not about objective truth or falsity, but more generally about coherence between mappings.

The view I present in this chapter is very much the same for conditionals in general. The case in which *if. . . then* connectives are used for logical purposes (truth and falsity) is only one instance of the more general notion of coherence of mappings as constrained by mental-space connections and matching conditions. Cornulier (1985) gives a convincing unitary analysis of *if*, based on general pragmatic principles, which ties in nicely with the present view.

Similar points can be made in connection with "metalinguistic conditionals" (Dancygier 1992; Dancygier and Sweetser 1996). For example, in English your father's cousin would usually be called your cousin. In some parts of Spain, the kinship system might have your father's brother and your father's cousin both called *tio*. As the most salient English counterpart of *tio* is *uncle,* a speaker addressing you and mentioning your father's cousin can say:

If we were speaking Spanish, he'd be your uncle.

In the Foundation Space, "speaking Spanish" triggers kinship realignments, which are elaborated in the Expansion Space using prototype correspondences with English (*tio–uncle*). The Matching Condition and Expansion Space are used to say something about kinship labeling *in Spanish,* by setting up a coherent network of fairly elaborate mappings (see Dancygier and Sweetser 1996 for a complete discussion, with appropriate diagrams). They are not set up to establish logical connections between speaking a particular language and being related to a particular person.

Chapter 6
Blends

Thought and language, I have been arguing, depend among other things on our capacity to manipulate webs of mappings between mental spaces. This book started out with general evidence for such mappings and went on to the local construction of spaces and connections in everyday discourse, including the elaborate tense and mood systems that language uses to guide us through mazes of interconnected spaces. In Chapter 4, we saw another dimension of the cognitive operations we perform on such structures: the analogical links and inference transfers within space configurations. All forms of thought are creative in the sense that they produce new links, new configurations, and correspondingly, new meaning and novel conceptualization. In this chapter, I give an overview of one important cognitive process that drives some of this creativity and depends crucially on cognitive mappings between mental spaces. The process, conceptual blending, is studied in some detail in Fauconnier and Turner (1994, 1995), Turner and Fauconnier (1995, 1996), Coulson (1995), and Mandelblit (1994, 1995).

1. Principles of Blending

Blending is in principle a simple operation, but in practice gives rise to myriad possibilities. It operates on two Input mental spaces to yield a third space, the *blend*. The blend *inherits partial structure* from the input spaces and *has emergent structure* of its own. Here are some of the conditions that are satisfied when two Input spaces I_1 and I_2 are blended:

(1) CROSS-SPACE MAPPING: There is a *partial* mapping of counterparts between the input spaces I_1 and I_2, as shown in Fig. 6.1.

(2) GENERIC SPACE: There is a *generic space,* which maps onto each of the inputs. This generic space reflects some common, usually more abstract, structure and organization shared by the inputs and defines the core cross-space mapping between them, as in Fig. 6.2.

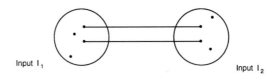

Figure 6.1.

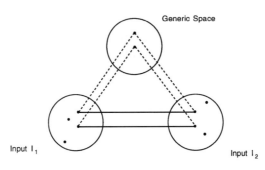

Figure 6.2.

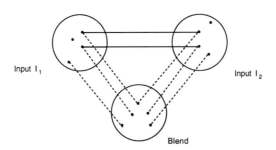

Figure 6.3.

(3) BLEND: The inputs I_1 and I_2 are partially projected onto a fourth space, the blend (see Fig. 6.3).

(4) EMERGENT STRUCTURE: The blend has emergent structure not provided by the inputs. This happens in three (interrelated) ways:

COMPOSITION: Taken together, the projections from the inputs make new relations available that did not exist in the separate inputs.

COMPLETION: Knowledge of background frames, cognitive and cultural models, allows the composite structure projected into the blend from the Inputs to be viewed as part of a larger self-contained structure

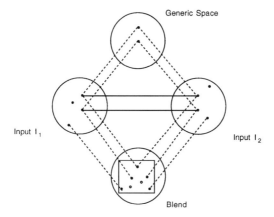

Figure 6.4.

in the blend. The pattern in the blend triggered by the inherited structures is "completed" into the larger, emergent structure.

ELABORATION: The structure in the blend can then be elaborated. This is "running the blend." It consists in cognitive work performed within the blend, according to its own emergent logic.

Schematically, then, a full four-space blend looks like Fig. 6.4. above. In the diagram, the square stands for the emergent structure in the blend. The diagram is meant to indicate that when counterparts are projected into the blend, they may be fused into a single element or projected separately. An additional possibility, not reflected in the diagram, is that one of the counterparts is projected but not the other. We shall see examples of these possibilities in the following illustrations, analyzed in Fauconnier and Turner (1994, 1995).

Consider the following riddle (Koestler 1964):

Riddle of the Buddhist monk and the mountain: A Buddhist monk begins at dawn one day walking up a mountain, reaches the top at sunset, meditates at the top for several days, until one dawn when he begins to walk back to the foot of the mountain, which he reaches at sunset. Making no assumptions about his starting or stopping or about his pace during the trips, prove that there is a place on the path which he occupies at the same hour of the day on the two separate journeys.[1]

An elegant way of showing that there is indeed such a place, occupied at exactly the same time going up and going down, would be to imagine

1. A version of this riddle appears in Arthur Koestler, *The Act of Creation* (New York: Macmillan, 1964), 183–9; Koestler attributes the invention of the riddle to Carl Dunker.

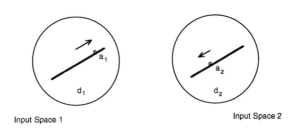

Input Space 1   Input Space 2

Figure 6.5.

the Buddhist monk walking both up and down the path on the same day. Then there must be a place where he meets himself, and that place is clearly the one he would occupy at the same time of day on the two separate journeys.

The riddle is solved, but there is a cognitive puzzle here. The situation that we devised to make the solution transparent is an utterly impossible and fantastic one. The monk cannot be making the two journeys simultaneously on the same day, and he cannot "meet himself." And yet this implausibility does not stand in the way of understanding the riddle and its solution. It is clearly disregarded. The situation imagined to solve the riddle is a blend: It combines features of the journey to the summit and of the journey back down, and uses emergent structure in that blend to make the affirmative answer apparent.

In mental-space terms, here is how this works. The two input spaces are the partial structures corresponding to the two journeys, as shown in Fig. 6.5. d_1 is the day of the upward journey, and d_2 the day of the downward journey; a_1 is the monk going up, a_2 is the monk going down. The cross-space mapping is straightforward. It connects the mountain, moving individual, day of travel, and motion in one space to the mountain, moving individual, day, and motion in the other space, as in Fig. 6.6.

The generic space contains what the inputs have in common: a moving individual and his position, a path linking foot and summit of the mountain, a day of travel. It does not specify the direction of motion or the actual day (see Fig. 6.7).

This configuration meets the conditions outlined above for projection into a fourth Blended space, Cross-Space Mapping and Generic Space. In the Blend, the two counterpart identical mountain slopes will be mapped onto a single slope. The two days of travel, d_1 and d_2, will be mapped onto a single day d' and therefore fused. But the moving

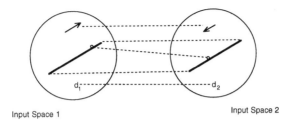

Input Space 1   Input Space 2

Figure 6.6.

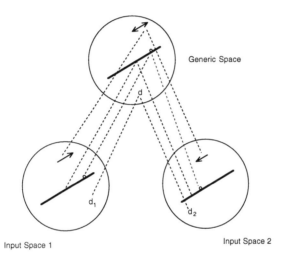

Figure 6.7.

individuals and their positions are mapped according to the time of day with direction of motion preserved, and therefore cannot be fused. Input 1 represents dynamically the entire upward journey, while Input 2 represents the entire downward journey. The rule for projection into a Blend preserves times and positions. The blend at time t of day d' contains a counterpart of a_1 at the position occupied by a_1 at time t of d_1, and a counterpart of a_2 at the position occupied by a_2 at time t of day d_2 (see Fig. 6.8).

The blend contains emergent structure not in the inputs. First by *composition*, for obvious reasons. There are now two moving individuals instead of one. They are moving in opposite directions, starting from opposite ends of the path, and their positions can be compared at any time of the trip, as they are traveling on the same day, d'. But this new

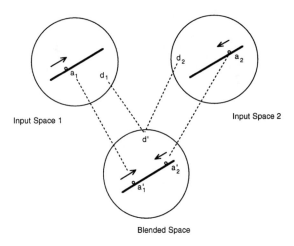

Figure 6.8.

structure can itself be viewed as a salient part of a familiar background frame: two people starting a journey at the same time from opposite ends of a path. By *completion*, this familiar structure is recruited into the blend. And we know, from "common sense," namely, familiarity with this background frame, that the two people will necessarily meet at some time t' of their journey.

Importantly, the blend remains hooked up to the inputs, so that structural properties of the blend can be mapped back onto the inputs. In our example, because of the familiarity of the frame obtained by completion, the inference that there is a meeting time t' with a common position p is completely automatic. The mapping back to the Input spaces yields as shown in Fig. 6.9. Because the rule adopted for mapping the individuals to the Blend preserves positions on the path, we "know" through this mapping that the positions of a_1 and a_2 are the "same" at time t' on the different days, simply because they are the same, by definition, in the frame of two people meeting, instantiated in the blend by their counterparts a'_1 and a'_2.

It is worth emphasizing that the pragmatic incongruity in the blend of the same person traveling in two opposite directions and meeting himself is disregarded, because the focus of the problem is on the meeting point and its counterparts in the input spaces. Blends are used cognitively in flexible ways. In other examples examined in Fauconnier and Turner (1994) and in Coulson (1995), similar incongruities in the blend

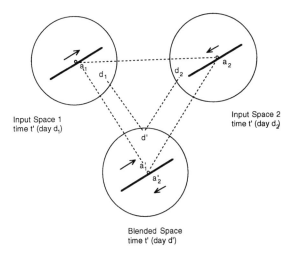

Figure 6.9.

get highlighted and mapped back to the Inputs for inferential and emotional effect.

Notice also that, in this blend, some counterparts have been fused (the days, the path on the different days, and the corresponding times on different days), whereas others have been projected separately (the monk on the way up, and the monk on the way down, the directions of motion). Projection from the Inputs is only partial: the specific dates of the journeys are not projected, nor the fact that the monk will stay at the top for a while after his upward journey. But the blend has new "emergent" structure not in the inputs: two moving individuals whose positions can be compared and may coincide, and the richer frame of two travelers going in opposite directions on the same path and necessarily meeting each other. This emergent structure is crucial to the performance of the reasoning task.

The Buddhist monk example presents a very salient and intuitively apparent blend, precisely because of its pragmatic anomaly. But our claim is that blends abound in all kinds of cases that go largely unnoticed. Some are created as we talk, others are conventional, and others are even more firmly entrenched in the grammatical structure. One example we discuss at some length, the "boat-race example," involves a modern catamaran *Great America II* sailing from San Francisco to Boston in 1993 and being compared to a clipper, *Northern Light*, that did the same run back in 1853. A few days before the catamaran reached Boston, observers were able to say:

At this point, Great America II *is 4.5 days ahead of* Northern Light.

This expression frames the two boats as sailing on the same course during the same time period in 1993. It blends the event of 1853 and that of 1993 into a single event. All the conditions outlined above for blending obtain. There is a cross-space mapping that links the two trajectories, the two boats, the two time periods, positions on the course, and so on. Projection to the blend from the Inputs is partial: The 1853 date is dropped, as are the 1853 weather conditions, the purpose of the trip, and so on. But the blend has rich emergent structure: Like the traveling monks, the boats are now in a position to be compared, so that one can be "ahead" of the other. This structure itself, two boats moving in the same direction on the same course and having departed from San Francisco on the same day, fits into an obvious and familiar cultural frame, that of a *race*. This yields additional emergent structure by *completion*. The race frame in the blend may be invoked more explicitly, as in:

At this point, Great America II *is barely maintaining a 4.5-day lead over* Northern Light.

"Maintaining a lead" is an intentional part of a race. Although in reality the catamaran is sailing alone, and the clipper's run took place 140 years before, the situation is described in terms of the blended space, in which, so to speak, the two boats left San Francisco on the same day in 1993 and are engaged in a race to Boston. As in the Buddhist monk example, no one is fooled into thinking that the clipper has magically reappeared. The blend remains solidly linked to the inputs into which inferences from the blend can be imported back, in particular the speeds and positions of the two boats on their respective runs many years apart. Another noteworthy property of the race frame in the blend is its emotional content. Sailors in a race are driven by emotions linked to winning, leading, losing, gaining, and so forth. This emotional value can be projected to Input 2. The solitary run of *Great America II* is conceived, thanks to the blend, as a race against the nineteenth-century clipper and can be lived with corresponding emotions.

The attested report that prompted our interest in the "boat race" was actually a magazine article in *Latitude* that contained the following: "As

we went to press, Rich Wilson and Bill Biewenga were barely maintaining a 4.5 day lead over the ghost of the clipper *Northern Light, . . .*"
The blend here has become reified. An explicit referent, the ghost, is
set up for the opponent of *Great America II* in the blended space. The
mapping is more extensive, although still implicit. "Ghost" allows the
projection from Input 1 that the clipper no longer (i.e., in 1993) exists.
But the starting times are still fused, and it is understood that the "ghost"
is retracing the exact run of the record-holding clipper. Again, nobody
is fooled into confusing the blend with reality. There is no inference that
the sailors actually saw a ghost ship, or even imagined one. The construction and operation of the blend is creative, but also conventional in
the sense that readers know immediately and without conscious effort
how to interpret it.

   The central features of blending, exemplified by the above examples,
are cross-space mapping, partial projection from inputs, generic space,
integration of events, and emergent structure through composition, completion, and elaboration.

   Here is another type of example that is common in everyday discourse,
from Fauconnier and Turner (1995), the "great debate." A philosophy
professor is lecturing to students or talking to colleagues and says: "I
claim that reason is a self-developing capacity. Kant disagrees with me
on this point. He says it's innate, but I answer that that's begging the
question, to which he counters, in *Critique of Pure Reason,* that only
innate ideas have power. But I say to that, what about neuronal group
selection? And he gives no answer." In the article, we describe the cognitive process as follows:

In one input mental space, we have the modern philosopher, making claims. In
a separate but related input mental space, we have Kant, thinking and writing.
In neither input space is there a debate. These two input spaces share frame
structure, which constitutes a generic space: there is a thinker, who has claims
and musings, a mode of expression, a particular language, and so on. The fourth
space, the blend, has both the modern philosopher (from the first input space)
and Kant (from the second input space). The blend recruits the frame of debate,
framing Kant and the modern philosopher as engaged in simultaneous debate,
mutually aware, using a single language to treat a recognized topic. The debate
frame comes up easily in the blend, through pattern completion, since so much
of its structure is already in place in the two inputs. Once the blend is established,
we can operate cognitively within that space, which allows us to manipulate the
various events as an integrated unit. The debate frame brings with it conventional

expressions, available for our use. We know the connection of the blend to the input spaces, and the way that structure or inferences developed in the blend translates back to the input spaces. We work over all four spaces simultaneously, but the blend gives us structure, integration, and efficiency not available in the other spaces.

A "realist" interpretation of the passage would be quite fantastic, like the monk and regatta cases. The philosophy professor and Kant would have to be brought together in time, would have to speak the same language, and so on. Again, no one is fooled into thinking that is the intent of the passage. In fact, using a debate blend of this type is so conventional that it will go unnoticed. And yet it has all the criterial properties of blending. There is a *cross-space mapping* linking Kant and his writings to the philosophy professor and his lecture. Counterparts include: Kant and the professor, their respective languages, topics, claims, times of activity, goal (e.g., search for truth), modes of expression (writing versus speaking). There is *partial projection to the blend:* Kant, the professor, some of their ideas, search for truth, are projected. Kant's time, language, mode of expression, the fact that he is dead, the fact that he was never aware of the future existence of our professor, are not projected. There is *integration of Events:* Kant's ideas and the professor's claims are integrated into a unified event, the debate. There is *emergent structure* through *composition:* We have two people talking in the same place at the same time. There is *emergent structure* through *completion:* Two people talking in the same place at the same time evoke the Cultural Frame of a conversation, a debate (if they are philosophers), an argument. This frame, the Debate Frame, structures the blend and is reflected by the syntax and vocabulary of the professor (*disagrees, answer, counters, what about, . . .*).

2. Counterfactual Blends

Now recall the analogical counterfactuals discussed in Chapter 4. It is easy to see that they too are structured as blends. The analogical mapping behind *In France, Watergate wouldn't have done Nixon any harm* was discussed at some length. It links prominent aspects of the American and French political systems. Presidents in each country are counterparts, voters in each country are counterparts, and so on. There is an input space for the U.S.A. and one for France. The generic space that guides this analogical mapping is a straightforward frame of political organization (labeled "Western democracy" frame in Chapter 4). So we have a *cross-space mapping* of counterparts such as Nixon and Mitterrand, and a *generic space* reflecting some partial schematic structure shared by the inputs. The counterfactual space that the sentence prompts us to build is a *blend* of the two inputs. It inherits the generic frame from both inputs, and the specific additional political and social properties of France from Input 2, by virtue of the space builder *in France*. These properties are not explicitly stated, however. They are just assumed to be projected from the "France" input space. From Input 1 (the U.S.A.), we get Nixon as president and Watergate as the current scandal. But, as in other blends, only partial projection is possible. In the projection, Nixon loses his American characteristics (English language, status as former vice-president, etc.). They are overridden (at least under one interpretation) by strong constraints on the French political system (the president speaks French, is French, etc.). Watergate, similarly, loses most of its specific geographical and American characteristics. It becomes a French scandal with relevant properties analogical to those of the American scandal. As explained earlier, the power of this construction comes from the projection from the blend back to the Inputs. Because Nixon in France does not suffer the same fate as his real counterpart, there must be properties of the structure projected from Input 2 that account for the difference. The invited inference, and intended meaning, of the statement is that a crucial difference between Input 2 (the French social and political system) and Input 1 (the American system) is responsible for the difference of consequences in the blend. And so we obtain the disanalogy.

As in mental-space constructions generally, there is a considerable amount of underspecification in this process. First, even if the above reading is selected by favoring the exportation into the blend of structural features of Input 2 over special characteristics of Nixon and Watergate, there is no indication of *what* aspects of the French system, society, mentality, and so on, are responsible for the difference. There is no really precise indication of the properties of Nixon in the blend that come from Input 1 rather than Input 2. All this is negotiable in further elaborations of the conversation. For instance, although the pragmatically salient interpretation of the construction is that the French have more tolerance for presidents' doing certain Watergate-like things, or for scandals in general, one could easily, with the same general blend, develop radically different extensions:

In France, Watergate wouldn't have done Nixon any harm because French presidents are more careful and never get caught when they rob their opponents' headquarters.

In France, Watergate wouldn't have done Nixon any harm because French presidents have the constitutional duty to search all political party headquarters once a year.

And so on, ad infinitum. All of these interpretations would still be using the blend described above.

Second, many other blends are compatible with the original sentence. Personal characteristics of Nixon or Watergate may be projected from Input 1, blocking projections from Input 2. The following extensions would invite such blends.

In France, Watergate wouldn't have done Nixon any harm because Nixon is loved by the French.

In France, Watergate wouldn't have done Nixon any harm because French presidents are not affected by U.S. scandals.

In France, Watergate wouldn't have done Nixon any harm because spying on American political parties is supported by public opinion.

In France, Watergate wouldn't have done Nixon any harm because he would never have been elected president in the first place.

And so on, and so forth. In all of these and similar extensions, different projections have been made from the inputs. They can all be used to make truth-conditionally completely different points: that Nixon is popular in France; that Western democracies spy on each other; that because people like Nixon don't get elected in France, there are no major political scandals. And this is not just implicature or hints. To understand the sentence in context is to have some idea of the kind of blend intended. But it may take a lot of elaboration for speaker and hearer to converge on sufficiently similar constructions. And, then again, there is no need for convergence. The folk-theoretical illusion that each expression of language has a meaning that we all retrieve in basically the same way allows interlocutors to interact under the impression of mutual comprehension, when in fact they may be engaged in quite different mental-space constructions. Analogical counterfactuals are a case in point.

Recall, as another case of counterfactual blending, examples mentioned in Chapter 1, like:

If I were you, I would hire me.

The meaning of such expressions involves a mapping from a reality space, where "you" is doing the hiring, to a counterfactual space in which the speaker's dispositions, but not her/his situation have been transferred to the addressee *you*. The space connection between speaker in reality and the addressee in the counterfactual allows the counterfactual employer to be identified as "*I*" by virtue of the Access Principle. Such counterfactuals are also clearly analogical. They invite an analogical interpretation in an intuitively obvious way: Compare the present situation in which *you* are doing the hiring to one in which *I* am in your place, confronted with the same decisions to make and the same candidates. Then export some features (like "whom I would hire") from one situation to the other. However, what we find in the linguistic expression *I would hire me* cannot be a reflection of either one of these situations. It is not being suggested that the employer should hire herself, or that the employee should take power and hire himself. The linguistic expression signals a blend, which has been set up by the cross-space analogical mapping between the two situations. In the blend we find partial projection of Input 1, the employer and the employee (*me*) being hired, and partial projection of Input 2, the speaker's dispositions and decisions. Diagrammatically, the construction is shown in Fig. 6.10.

$\mathfrak{A}$ is the analogical connector, and $\mathfrak{I}$ is the identity connector. In the analogy (Input 2), the speaker (I) becomes the employer. The worker b_2 is "like" its counterpart b_1, but not explicitly specified. In the blend, the employer (I) is projected from Input 2, the worker (also I) is projected from Input 1, and the employer hires the worker. This is explicitly specified by the counterfactual expression *I would hire me*.

Now, the entire configuration can be exploited to yield inferences. If the pragmatic principle P_1 of "egocentric attribution" ("do what I do"—see Chapter 1) is covertly invoked, then the structure in the blend maps back to Input 1: The addressee should hire the speaker. By P_1, the blended structure (a' HIRE b') is desirable, and therefore its counterpart in "reality" (Input 1) is desirable: a_1 HIRE b_1.

The same blend can be used to make different points. The speaker, Joe, might be commenting on his own stupidity: I, Joe, am stupid enough

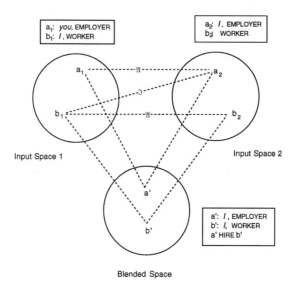

Figure 6.10.

that, if I were the employer, I would hire Joe. The blend here would be enriched by the additional background frame that it is clearly stupid to hire Joe. It would follow, in the blend, that Joe is stupid (because he hires Joe), and this feature (of element a') would be transferred (via a_2) to its identity counterpart b_1 in the reality Input 1. As Coulson (1995) has shown, once several spaces are connected, a blend can be used to transfer inferences in either direction. The stupidity of a' derived in the blend is attributed to a_2 by projection to Input 2, and then in turn to b_1 by identity.

Notice that, as in the Buddhist monk example, there is no problem with two individuals, the employer and worker, being identical in the blend, because there are still two distinct space elements, which happen to be linked by connectors to the same element in the original Input 1.

As in so many of the examples reviewed in this book, a striking feature of the blended construction is its underspecification. Although there are strong constraints on blending, which I shall recapitulate below, there is no recipe for knowing what will be projected from the inputs and what will be projected back. In that respect the system is very flexible. So consider a radically different projection scheme based on the same blended configuration. The speaker says, *If I were you, the company would hire me right away*. This is likely to mean that the addressee,

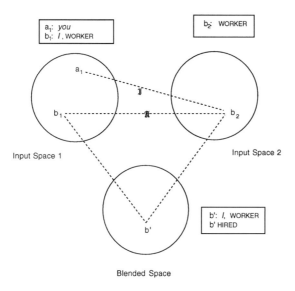

Figure 6.11.

not the speaker, is the sort of person who would get hired. The analogical cross-space mapping that underlies the blend is constructed in
a different way than before. Instead of "I" replacing "you" in the relevant frame of hiring, it is the other way around: "you" replaces "I" as
the worker looking for employment. In the blend, the individual under
scrutiny (element b') inherits his frame properties (worker) from "I"
(element b_1 in Input 1), and some of his identity (e.g., social status or
professional competence) from "you" (element b_2 in Input 2), as shown
in Fig. 6.11.

In this case also, inferences will be made in the blend and exported
to the inputs. One pragmatic possibility is to focus on the disanalogy
between Input 1 and the blend: The worker gets hired in the latter, but
not the former. As the frame is the same, the difference is due to individual properties. In the blend, b' has properties of b_2, which are in
turn properties of a_1. The inference is that the absence of such properties prevents the speaker from getting hired. What they are is anybody's
guess, out of context: the addressee's talent, or social connections, or
nifty clothes. . . . Although we talk here of underspecification, there is no
vagueness in the construction itself. The participants in the conversation
are prompted grammatically to construct a blend, to find contextually
relevant features that produce inferences, and to export such inferences

via the connectors. The rich meaning that will ensue is not inherently contained in the grammatical structures. What the grammar does is specify a range of constructions of blends from which to choose and on which to elaborate. This is why language functions so differently from codes, logical truth-conditional systems, and the like. It never does more than set a very schematic stage for the meaning that is going to be built and negotiated locally in usage.

Blends often go unnoticed. They are constructed automatically and often conventionally, as in the example of the catamaran being 4.5 days ahead of the clipper, when in fact the boats are separated by a number of decades. But blends can also be used very overtly, as in the Buddhist monk case, and they can serve outlandish purposes. Recall the exchange between Victoria and Webster in Chapter 4, and Victoria's subsequent remark:

You know that sister Webster doesn't have. Well, she doesn't know how lucky she is.

A number of spaces are invoked. Webster, in the previous dialogue, had built a counterfactual N in which he had a sister who could not possibly be a hooker. In the Base, he had no sister. Victoria is constructing a blend of the Base B and the Counterfactual N, for purely local reasoning purposes; the blend inherits the "sister" from counterfactual space N, but also inherits the property that she is not Webster's sister from the Base. In the blend, she is lucky (and doesn't know it); in N, she is Webster's sister, and therefore unlucky. The disanalogy between N and the blend (sister/unlucky $\neq$ not-sister/lucky) yields the desired inferences that it is a very good thing not to be Webster's sister, and by implication that Webster is extremely obnoxious indeed. The blend solution has the added advantage of avoiding the introduction of fictitious elements into the Base—a shortcoming of the initial treatment considered in Chapter 4.

Blends allow very generally for what Talmy (1995) calls *fictive* constructions, which are cognitively efficient because they remain linked to the relevant input spaces, so that inferences, emotions, and such can be transferred back and forth. "Fictivity" is a crucial component of cognition and shapes everyday thought—scientific and artistic alike. I shall now review briefly the operation of blending in a variety of modes of thought. The issues are examined in far greater detail in Fauconnier and Turner (in preparation).

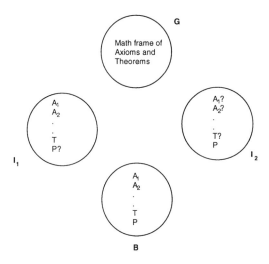

Figure 6.12.

3. Blends in Scientific Thought

3.1. Reductio

The common mathematical reasoning by "reductio" is a counterfactual blend. One seeks to prove "not P" and sets up a blend in which we have known axioms and theorems, and also P. We operate in the blend as we would in a well-formed mathematical space, until we reach a contradiction. The nonviability of the blend establishes the "truth" of "not P" in the original input.

The complete blend configuration looks something like Fig. 6.12. In Input 1, we have the axioms and relevant theorems of the mathematical system being used. In that space, P is not established; its status is unknown. In Input 2, P is true, but the axioms leading to P are not known. In the blend, known axioms and theorems are imported from Input 1, along with P, from Input 2. As in the general case of blending, we can "run the blend," to uncover its structure. In the case of reductio, the goal is to reveal the mathematical inconsistency of B by producing a contradiction in B. The blend is therefore "fictive": It does not correspond to a viable mathematical situation. The point of running the blend is to show that it cannot match Input 1 (see Chapter 5), and therefore that P does not hold in Input 1. And the reason it cannot match is that Input 1 is assumed to contain no contradiction.

3.2. When Failed Reductio Leads to Discovery

The power of blends lies in their emergent structure, and this emergent structure is revealed by "running the blend." We do not know in advance where such elaboration will lead. When Gerolamo Saccheri set out to prove Euclid's Fifth Postulate, he reasoned that although the postulate had eluded mathematical demonstration, it was clearly true on experiential and intuitive grounds. A reductio—assuming the falsity of the postulate—could therefore lead only to contradiction, and obtaining that contradiction would constitute a proof by reductio of the postulate. In effect, Saccheri constructed a blend in which the usual laws and axioms of geometry applied except for the Fifth Postulate itself, replaced by the axiom that, through a point P, there are at least two parallels to a line l.[2] Saccheri's purpose was a proof by reductio: The blend was intended to self-destruct mathematically. But this is not what happened; the blend turned out to be mathematically viable, and Saccheri's work became the basis for the development of non-Euclidean geometries.[3] Even more remarkably, it turned out that, far from being mere mathematical curiosities, such geometries could and did apply to our physical universe.

This example, which Turner and I view as typical of scientific and conceptual change, illustrates a deep property of blends in relation to creativity. They are not just conceptual constructions. They are genuine domains of mental exploration—running blends can lead to deep discoveries that were not anticipated in setting up the blend. Mathematicians did not start out with the intuition that there were non-Euclidean geometries waiting to be formalized. On the contrary, they were firmly convinced that geometry was inherently Euclidean, and the purpose of Saccheri's counterfactual blend was to establish this rigorously through reductio. Instead, what happened was that the blend took on a life of its own: It contained what its creator had not foreseen, "hyperbolic geometry," a radically novel conception of space, which Einstein and others would later apply to the physical universe.

3.3. Instruments of Conceptual Change

The example of hyperbolic geometry is not isolated. There is evidence that conceptual integration through blending has played a key role in

2. See Humbert 1957 and Kline 1980.
3. Saccheri himself mistakenly believed that his construction had led to a contradiction, and that he had succeeded in proving Euclid's postulate. Others later realized that a viable alternate geometry had emerged (Lambert, Gauss, Bolyai, and, later, Lobatchevsky and Riemann).

the development of science. In Fauconnier and Turner (1994), we look in some detail at the case of number theory in mathematics. Imaginary numbers first showed up in the formulas of sixteenth-century mathematicians Jerome Cardan and Raphael Bombelli. They were considered to be only notational expedients, with no conceptual basis ("sophistic," "imaginary," "impossible"). And even though John Wallis was able to provide a detailed geometric analogy for such numbers as early as 1685, one had to wait at least another century for a comprehensive mathematical theory of complex numbers that was conceptually acceptable to mathematicians. This emerging theory is a remarkable blend, in which numbers have properties of numbers (multiplication, addition, and so on) and also properties of points in space (or vectors), such as Cartesian coordinates and polar coordinates (angles and magnitudes). Operations in the blend are characterized in terms of the new conceptual structure. Multiplication, for instance, is the addition of angles and the product of magnitudes.

The emergence of the concept of complex numbers has all the formal properties of blending outlined in the first section of this chapter. An extended cross-space mapping links real and imaginary numbers to points in two-dimensional space. The seed for this mapping is the preexisting projection of numbers onto one-dimensional space (the "line" going from $-\infty$ to $+\infty$). A generic space contains the more abstract structure common to the domains of space and numbers. In the language of twentieth-century mathematics, this generic space is a commutative ring. Selective projection operates from the inputs into the blend, which inherits both spatial and arithmetic structure. The emergent structure in the blend is essentially that of operations on vectors/numbers. These operations are constrained by the standard rules of multiplication and addition inherited from the input of "numbers," but they acquire the additional interpretation of operations on angles (called "arguments") and magnitudes. The polar coordinates of numbers and the vectorial properties are emergent in the blend, as they were not part of the analogical cross-space mapping between points and numbers (based on Cartesian coordinates).

The emergence of theoretical concepts in physics displays a similar dynamics. Jeff Lansing has studied the diaries of Fourier and Maxwell, and offers substantial evidence that they were engaged in the construction of creative blended spaces. In developing his theory of heat propagation, Fourier first constructed a cross-space mapping between two inputs. One input had a metal ring with a flame applied at one point and thermometers measuring temperature at various other points. The other input would be a hollow, porous ring into which a fluid was forced through one orifice. The analogy that holds between these inputs and measurements of temperature and pressure constitutes a suitable cross-space mapping for a blend, which incorporates the notions of temperature and heat from one input, and the notion of liquid, volume, and pressure from the other. In the blend, we have the full-blown conception of heat as a fluid with specific properties of diffusion and propagation.

Lansing offers similar support for the idea that Maxwell's unification of theories of electricity, heat, magnetism, and galvanism is achieved through the conscious elaboration of a blend. Notice that the conception of heat as a fluid has been crucial to the development of physics, but that it has been replaced by a different conception based on molecular kinetics. When blends are successful, they become our new construal of reality, but the essence of scientific evolution is to move from one construal to the next. Change is permanent because blends are always elaborated, but we perceive major scientific shifts when novel blends are constructed.

What is so clearly apparent in science applies to conceptual change more generally—that is, to category formation, cultural models, and language itself (grammar and meaning). Fauconnier and Turner (1994 and in preparation) examine how the cognitive operation of conceptual integration and blending operates in this wider range of cases.

4. Blending and Metaphor

Metaphor is a salient and pervasive cognitive process that links conceptualization and language. It depends crucially on a cross-space mapping between two inputs (the Source and the Target). This makes it a prime candidate for the construction of blends, and indeed we find that blended spaces play a key role in metaphorical mappings. That is, in addition to the familiar Source and Target of metaphorical projection, blends are constructed in which important cognitive work gets accomplished.

The following excerpt from our article on blending and metaphor (Turner and Fauconnier forthcoming) illustrates this aspect of metaphor for the conventional expression "to dig one's own grave," which implies that a person is doing things that will lead to failure without being aware of it.

At first glance, what we have here is a straightforward projection from the concrete domain of graves, corpses, and burial to abstract domains of getting into trouble, unwittingly doing the wrong things, and ultimate failure. Failing is being dead and buried; bad moves that precede and cause failure are like actions (grave digging) that precede burial. It is foolish to facilitate one's own burial or failure; and it is foolish to be unaware of one's actions, especially when they lead to one's very extinction.

However, a closer look reveals extraordinary mismatches between the purported source and target of this metaphor. The *causal structure* is inverted. Foolish actions cause failure but grave digging does not cause death. It is typically someone's death that prompts others to dig a grave. And if the grave is atypically prepared in advance, to secure a plot, to keep workers busy, or because the person is expected to die, there is still not the slightest causal connection from the digging to the dying. The *intentional structure* does not carry over. Sextons do not dig graves in their sleep, unaware of what they are doing. In contrast, the figurative digging of one's own grave is conceived of as unintentional misdirection of actions. The *frame structure* of agents, patients, and sequence of events is not preserved. Our background knowledge is that the "patient" dies, and then the "agent" digs the grave and buries the "patient." But in the metaphor, the actors are fused and the ordering of events is reversed. The "patient" does the digging and, if the grave is deep enough, has no other option than to die and occupy it. Even in the improbable real-life case in which one might dig one's own grave in advance, there would be no necessary temporal connection between finishing the digging and perishing. The *internal event structure* does not match. In the target, it is certainly true that the more trouble you are in, the more you risk failure. Amount of trouble is mapped onto depth of grave. But, again, in the source there is no correlation between the depth of a person's grave and their chances of dying.

Now recall the rationale often proposed for metaphor: Readily available background or experiential structure and inferences of the source are recruited to understand the target. By that standard, and in view of the considerable mismatches, *digging one's own grave* should be a doomed metaphor. In fact, it's a very successful one.

This paradox dissolves when we consider, in addition to the source and target input spaces, the construction of the blended space. The blend inherits the concrete structure of graves, digging, and burial from the input source; but it inherits causal, intentional, and internal event structure from the input target. They are not simply juxtaposed. Rather, *emergent* structure specific to the blend is created. In the blend, all the curious properties noted above actually hold. The existence of a satisfactory grave causes death and is a necessary precondition for it. It follows straightforwardly that the deeper the grave, the closer it is to completion and the greater the chance for the grave's intended occupant to die. It follows that in the blend (as opposed to the source), digging one's grave is a grave mistake, as it makes dying more probable. In the blend, it becomes *possible* to be unaware of one's very concrete actions. This is projected from the target input, where it is indeed fully possible, and frequent, to be unaware of the significance of one's actions. But in the blend, it remains *highly foolish* to be unaware of such concrete actions; this is projected from the source input. And it will project back to the target input to produce suitable inferences (i.e., highlight the foolishness and misperception of an individual's behavior).

We wish to emphasize that in the construction of the blend, a single shift in causal structure, *the existence of a grave* causes *death* instead of *death* causes *the existence of a grave,* is enough to produce *emergent* structure, specific to the blend: the undesirability of digging one's grave, exceptional foolishness in not being aware of it, correlation of depth of grave with probability of death. The causal inversion is guided by the target, but the *emergent* structure is deducible within the blend from the new causal structure and familiar commonsense background knowledge. This point is essential, because the *emergent* structure, although "fantastic" from a literal interpretation point of view, is supremely efficient for the purpose of transferring the intended inferences back to the target input, and thereby making real-world inferences. This emergent structure is not in the inputs—it is part of the cognitive construction in the blend. But, also, it is not *stated* explicitly as part of the blend. It just follows, fairly automatically, from the unstated understanding that the causal structure has been projected from the target, not from the source.

The integration of events in the blend is indexed to events in both of the input spaces. We know how to translate structure in the blend to structure in the input spaces. The blend is an integrated platform for organizing and developing those other spaces. Consider a slightly fuller expression, "with each investment you make, you are digging your grave a little deeper." In the target, there are no graves but there are investments; in the source, the graves are not financial but one does dig; in the blend, investments are simultaneously instruments of digging, and what one digs is one's *financial grave*. A single action is simultaneously investing and digging; a single condition is simultaneously having finished the digging and having lost one's money. Digging your own grave does not kill you, but digging your own financial grave does cause your death/bankruptcy.

A different but related metaphor pointed out by George Lakoff (personal communication) illustrates the role of blends, and even multiple blends. A mother could say to her turbulent son, "You're driving me into my grave." Our experiential source domain of death, graves, and funerals does not by itself provide the structure we need to understand this projection. In real life, one is either not dead and not in a grave or dead and completely in a grave. In the target for this metaphor, on the other hand, there is a conception of "distance to death" correlated with aging, flagging powers, and so on. In the blend, this conception is projected from the target input, while the correlation of death with grave is projected from the source. The resulting emergent structure in the blend has features absent from both inputs. In the blend, one enters the grave progressively (cf. the idiom *to have one foot in the grave*), and different speeds of entry depend on external forces (*driving, pushing, ...*) and on internal resistance. The grave preexists (in contrast to the previous case, in which it was dug), and the path to the grave, and into it, is mapped onto the notion of "distance to death" in the target, which is itself metaphorical. Because of the double metaphor, the blend is multiple. There are three inputs: a space of graves and burial, a space of life with aging and progressive weakness, and a space of motion along a path. The integrated scene in the blend of someone being slowly pushed into a grave inherits structure selectively from all three.

5. Blends in Action and Design

Conceptual blending is not specifically linked to language use. It operates in many areas of cognition, including design and action.

A good example of blending in design, provided by Dan Gruen (personal communication), is the Macintosh desktop interface, which was constructed on the basis of two conceptual inputs, the input of more traditional computer commands, and the input of ordinary work in an office with a desk, files, and folders. A cross-space mapping matches computer files to paper files, directories to folders, accessing a directory to opening a folder, and so on. The generic space that mediates this mapping has a more schematic and abstract notion of information as contained in larger sets of information and movable from one set to another. In the blend, structure is selectively projected from the inputs, and we end up with coherent, integrated, emergent structure specific to the blend. There is no literal putting of anything into anything else, and there is no longer any mandatory typing of commands. This activity, however, is now partially structured in terms of familiar inputs, so that we can, with little effort, recruit the conceptual structure of office work to run the blend while understanding that we are executing computer commands; and yet none of the motor actions performed in the blend are the motor actions performed for its counterparts in the input of office work. Objectively, the integrated activity is totally novel, and yet it is immediately congenial and accessible, thanks to the massive projection from familiar inputs.

Novel action patterns often develop through blends, and sometimes are actually taught by explicitly invoking the blending. I remember a ski instructor who was trying to teach a novice to hold his arms correctly and look down the slope (rather than in the direction of the skis). He told the novice to imagine that he was a waiter in Paris carrying a tray with champagne and croissants. By focusing his attention on the tray in trying to avoid spilling the champagne, the novice was able to produce something approaching the right integrated motion on the slope. The inputs in this case are the ski situation and the restaurant situation, with arm and body positions mapped onto each other. The generic space has only human posture and motion, with no particular context. But in the blend, the skier is also actually carrying the champagne tray. The blend is of course a fantasy, but it does map the right motion back onto the ski input. Rather remarkably, this pedagogical feat requires no actual champagne and croissants. Just thinking of them is enough. During the learning stage, the novice has a very peculiar idea of what he is doing. But then, when the integration has succeeded, and the ski input has acquired the proper structure, through backward projection, the blend can be abandoned.

6. Blending and Grammar

Modern work in cognitive linguistics has focused on *grammatical constructions* (in Langacker's terms, symbolic assemblies), pairings of forms and meanings. Goldberg (1995), for instance, studies, among others, the Caused Motion Construction, which has the form "NP V NP PP," and the schematic meaning "a causes b to move to c by doing d," as in:

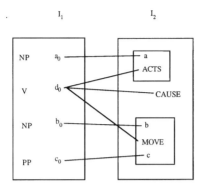

Figure 6.13.

The sergeant waved the tanks into the compound.

$$\begin{array}{cccc} \text{NP} & \text{V} & \text{NP} & \text{PP} \\ a & d & b & c \end{array}$$

Fauconnier and Turner (1996) and Mandelblit (1995b) show that such grammatical constructions are blends, which are entrenched but evolve diachronically. The general driving force behind this phenomenon is the linguistic pressure to represent complex integrations of events by making maximum use of existing grammatical constructions. In the Caused Motion case (Fig. 6.13), there are two inputs:

Input 1: the basic construction, found in many languages, a_0 b_0 c_0 d_0 where d_0 is an action (e.g., throwing, putting) that causes motion and transfer of b_0 from the agent a_0 to some location c_0. It is expressed in English through the syntactic form:

$$\begin{array}{cccc} \text{NP} & \text{V} & \text{NP} & \text{PP} \end{array}$$

[as in *John throws the ball to Susan*].

Input 2: a causal sequence of the form:

[[a ACTS] CAUSES [b MOVE to c]].

A cross-space mapping between Inputs 1 and 2 will naturally match a, b, c with a_0, b_0, c_0, respectively. Verbs in the basic construction (like *throw*) contain all in one, the agent's action, the object's motion, and the causative link between the two. d_0 (in I_1) may therefore map to either ACT, CAUSE, or MOVE in I_2. This allows three blends in English; all three inherit their syntactic structure from Input 1, and their conceptual

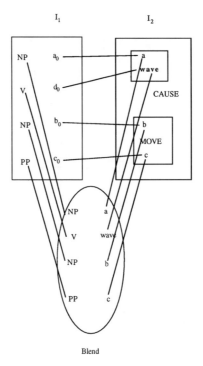

Figure 6.14.

structure from Input 2. If d_0 is mapped onto the agent's action (ACT) in I_2, we get examples like: *The sergeant waved the tanks into the compound* (see Fig. 6.14). The verb *wave* is not intrinsically a causative. In the Blend, it is projected from Input 2, with the structural position of its counterpart d_0 in Input 1. The causal connection between the waving and the tanks' motion, and the tanks' motion itself, are left unspecified.

If we map d_0 onto the object's motion (MOVE) in I_2, we get examples like: *Junior sped the car around the Christmas tree* (see Fig. 6.15). In this example, the agent's action and the causal link are left unspecified, while the object's motion is highlighted. Syntactically, the verb *speed* ends up in the same position as *wave* in the previous case or *throw* in the prototypical case.

Finally, the causal link, and not the action or the motion, may be highlighted, as in:

The sergeant <u>let</u> the tanks into the compound.

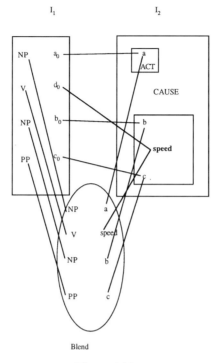

Blend

Figure 6.15.

This corresponds to a cross-space mapping of d_0 onto the CAUSE component of the conceptual sequence, expressed here by the English verb *let*.

Notice that in all these cases, we need the full construction of the
blend. It is not the case that verbs like *wave, let, speed* have simply been
independently extended:

*The sergeant waved the tanks.
*Junior sped the car.
*The sergeant let the tanks.

Compare with:

The boy threw the ball.

The verb *throw* functions as a transitive verb independently of the caused
motion construction.

The extension of the basic construction through blending is specific to
some languages like English. This particular blend contains no syntactic

innovation, in the sense that the syntactic structure is imported from one of the inputs without modification. It does represent semantic innovation, allowing for a range of novel integrated conceptions like:

The psychic will think your husband into another galaxy.
They prayed the boys home. [news item about two missing boys]
Frankenstein choked the life out of Dracula. [It is Dracula, not the life, that is getting choked, but the blend operates on an input with metaphorical motion of life out of Dracula's body.]

Grammatical blending is powerful and creative. In many cases more complex than the one outlined above, emergent syntactic structure arises in the blend along with emergent conceptual structure. This is shown for causatives in French by Fauconnier and Turner (1996), and in much more detail for a systematic range of causative constructions in Hebrew, by Mandelblit (1995b). Mandelblit shows how basic transitive and transfer constructions in one input are projected to the blend, which also displays causative verbal morphology. Different morphological patterns are available in Hebrew, depending on which aspect of the input causal sequence is highlighted.

Lisa Hogan (1995) has studied a grammatical blend in English that is in the process of becoming entrenched and grammatical with some younger speakers (average writers among undergraduate students at the University of New Mexico; the construction appears with an average frequency of 15 sentences in 500 pages of writing). Examples of the blend are:

By being able to send messages on the telephone helped make life better.
By the way elections are sequenced every four years prevents one party from gaining permanent control.
By Stephen King's not growing up in a lonely environment might have changed his fondness for horror.

Instead of the standard subject NP's (*Being able...*, *The way the elections...*, *Stephen King's not...*) we find prepositional phrases introduced by *by*. Conceptually, the new construction is able to carry the additional information that the subject NP is a means for somebody. Syntactically, we have a novel structure with a *by*-phrase in subject position. This structure is heartily rejected by a majority of speakers who have not (yet?) developed the blend in their own speech.

7. Fictive Motion

Talmy (forthcoming), Langacker (1987), and Matsumoto (forthcoming) have studied fictive (or abstract, or subjective) motion phenomena, exemplified by sentences like:

(*a*)   *The blackboard goes all the way to the wall.*
(*b*)   *The cliff faces away from the valley.*

Typically, such examples reflect stationary scenes but use expressions linked to motion in order to do so (*goes . . . to* in (*a*), *away from* in (*b*)). This works by having an "imaginary" trajector move along the relevant dimension of an object, or along some "imaginary" path linking two objects. The expressions are not metaphorical; (*a*) cannot be interpreted as a literal motion of a blackboard in a source domain that would project onto a "stationary" target domain. What moves fictively is not the blackboard but the imaginary trajector. This is a remarkable mode of expression: It conveys motion and immobility at the same time. Objective immobility is expressed along with perceptual or conceptual motion (the conceptualizer's gaze, mental scanning, or structure projection).[4] This apparent contradiction is a consequence of conceptual blending, which, as we have seen, allows several connected but heterogeneous spaces to be maintained simultaneously within a single mental construction.

The two inputs to the blend are a space with a moving trajector on a path, with a reference point and a space for the stationary scene described in Fig. 6.16. The path in Input 1 is mapped onto the relevant dimension of the object (blackboard) in Input 2. This is determined by context combined with typical functional and geometric properties of the object (or set of objects). Accordingly, the choice of a relevant dimension can vary:

The blackboard goes all the way to the ceiling.
The blackboard extends diagonally all the way to the righthand
  corner.

The reference point in Input 1 maps onto an object or location in Input 2. The trajector has no counterpart, and the object itself has no counterpart in Input 1. In the blend, the two partial input structures are projected as shown in Fig. 6.17. In the blend, there is motion, and the blackboard

4. In some cases (*The road goes from Paris to Orléans*), the object described (the road) is associated with moving objects (vehicles) by background knowledge. In others, it is natural to link the fictive motion with an observer's visual scanning (*I can see all the way to Alcatraz*). But, as Talmy observes, this doesn't have to be the case (*The mountain range goes from Canada to Mexico*).

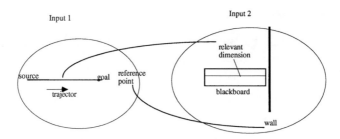

Figure 6.16.

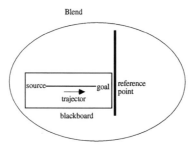

Figure 6.17.

has become a trajectory. A general metonymy allows the descriptions for trajectories to identify their typical trajectors:

The road climbs slowly to the top of the hill.
After you take the turn, the road takes about ten minutes to reach the
    ridge.
Max was an hour ahead of schedule. [The schedule is a metaphoric
    trajectory (see Chapter 1, section 2.2.3).]

The sentence *The blackboard goes all the way to the wall* applies literally to the blend, with *the blackboard* identifying its typical trajector (projected from Input 1). The blend, of course, remains hooked up to the original inputs, so that inferences made from the scene with motion can be mapped back appropriately to Input 2 (the stationary scene). The inference in the blend that the goal coincides with the reference point projects back to Input 2, yielding the inference that one end of the blackboard is located against the wall.

A little more explicitly:

from I_1: trajector moves from source to goal;

by cross–space mapping and projection to the blend: goal is one end of the
  blackboard, along the horizontal dimension, reference point for fictive motion
  is the wall;
by elaboration in the blend: goal, edge of blackboard, reference point, and
  wall are colocated;
by projection back to I_2: the edge of the blackboard is against the wall.

Talmy (forthcoming) insightfully distinguishes many types of fictive
motion and corresponding paths and trajectories (access, advent, cov-
erage, etc.). Emanation paths that go from one object to another are
especially interesting. Talmy gives examples like:

The snake is lying toward the TV.

Superficially, stationary vocabulary (*lying*) is combined with motion
vocabulary (*toward*). The first comes from Input 2, indicating a stationary, oriented position. The second comes from Input 1 (the trajector
moves toward the reference point). In the blend, we have a trajector
moving toward the TV on an emanation path originating at the position
of the snake.

Metaphorical fictive motion is also conceptual blending. Recall the
examples studied in Chapter 1, section 2.2.3:

I can't catch up with myself.
I'm getting ahead of myself.

They involve metaphorical motion along a schedule of events, and
metaphorical motion through time. Input 1, the "source" space, has an
individual moving along a path. The path projects onto two ordered sets
in Input 2: the time scale and the event scale (see Fig. 6.18). The position
of source trajector i projects onto t_k, the actual time for the individual
in the target, and onto E_j, the event on the schedule that the individual
is actually engaged in. t_j and t_k are respectively the scheduled times for
events E_j and E_k.

In the blend, the two scales are projected onto the same simple path of
motion, their counterpart from Input 1 as shown in Fig. 6.19. It follows
that in the blend the same individual is in two places at once, when (in
Input 2) the schedule of events is not followed properly.

Parallel to the "blackboard" example, we also find:

I'm ahead of (or *behind*) *schedule.*

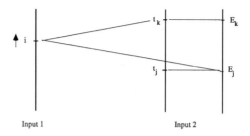

Figure 6.18.

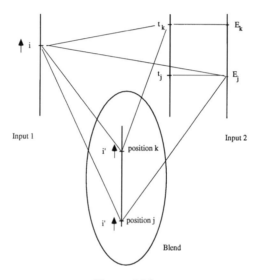

Figure 6.19.

Schedule (the metaphorical trajectory) is linked to the trajector on the scale of events, and so the word *schedule* serves to identify this trajector in the blend. In the blend, the individual's position is compared to the "schedule-trajector's" position. This projects back to Input 2, yielding the objective information regarding the events scheduled and the events actually engaged in.

Here again, what is noteworthy is the emergent structure in the blend and the conceptualization to which it gives rise. In Input 1, there is only one moving individual. In Input 2, we have two abstract ordered scales of times and events. But in the blend, we have two moving individuals on the same path. This allows pattern completion to operate. Two moving individuals on the same path fit into the more structured frame of a race. And so, the "racing" construal can be projected to the abstract cultural construction of events and schedules. This explains the use of vocabulary like *catch up, keep up, fall behind* that is found in such examples.

Again, we note that the complexity and richness of such constructions cannot be accounted for by direct source–target metaphors. In particular, it is impossible, in the source domain of racing, for an individual to be at two places at the same time or to be running against herself.

8. Creativity in Everyday Life

Many blends become entrenched and can then be used without novel manipulation of the links to the original inputs. This is the case, presumably, for the grave-digging metaphor, the boat-race example in its simple form (*being 4.5 days ahead*), or the computer desktop, once it has been learned as a self-contained activity. The same is true of grammatical constructions in their most standard uses (*kick the ball over the fence*).

But in everyday action and speech we also perform significant "creative" on-line blending. A linguistic form may contain multiple clues that a blend is in order, without specifying the actual selective projection from the inputs or the emergent structure in the blend. This was apparent in all the counterfactual examples in section 2 above. To understand the *Nixon* example or the *if I were you* examples correctly, one needs to construct an appropriate analogical mapping between inputs and then selectively project to a blended space. As noted above, and in Chapter 1, there are typically many ways to do this that will be compatible with the purely linguistic instructions provided. Building the "right" blend depends highly on context and available background. For instance, in the *Nixon* example, we need to know the point of the conversation: Are we interested in political systems, in the individual Nixon, in people's nationalities? What do we know about Watergate, France, Western democracies? How do we run the blend, once initial choices of selective projection and cross-space mapping have been made? And how does running the blend interact with later selective projection? From a strictly formal point of view, the number of possibilities is staggering. And yet, what we have here is banal everyday conversation. The point, reiterated over and over in this book, but perhaps even more apparent in the case of conceptual blending, is that we engage in cognitively creative activity whenever we assign meanings to linguistic forms. Even at the most elementary level of meaning construction, the creative power of intricate cognitive operations is essential.

Understanding is creating. To communicate is to trigger dynamic creative processes in other minds and in our own. The mappings we have studied in this book can be entrenched (as in conventional metaphor and established grammatical constructions), but they also operate on-line to yield novel meanings, construals and interpretations. In fact, entrenched mappings provide strong background support for on-line innovations. Seana Coulson (personal communication) reports the following excerpt from a newspaper editorial:

The U.S. is in a position to exhume itself from the shallow grave that we've dug for ourselves.

This comment on the political situation takes advantage of the conventional grave-digging metaphorical blend mentioned in section 4 above. It does so by means of an elaborate novel blend, in which the depth of the grave is mapped onto the seriousness of the difficulties, and the grave digger is also the dead individual, who resurrects by being exhumed. The conventional grave-digging blend, with its intricate emergent structure, is available as a background mapping for constructing the novel and even more elaborate blend required to make sense of the sentence.

Metaphors produced and understood in everyday conversation often have this dimension of creativity in addition to the exploitation of conventionally entrenched conceptual mappings. Fauconnier and Turner (1994) discuss the following example, a comment made by 1992 presidential candidate Tom Harkin about rival George Bush.

George Bush was born on third base and thinks he hit a triple.

A conventional projection from sports to life is exploited here. It is based on the general schema of agents in competition, striving to reach goals, to gain rank, and so on. But in the blend, we find novel, peculiar, structure. Social life and baseball are merged, birth takes place on bases, and players can be fantastically deluded as to what is going on in the game. This allows for inferences not available in the inputs of baseball and social life. For instance, one central inference of this sentence is that George Bush is not just stupid in the expected ways we all are stupid, but to a much higher, "inconceivable" degree. Where does the inference come from? We give the following account:

It is not available from the source, because although there is more than one way to get on base (the batter can be walked, a pinch runner can be put on, and so on), in none of them is it possible to be confused about how you got on base. There is stupidity in baseball, of remarkable kinds, such as those sampled in bloopers films, and standard kinds, such as mental errors in the execution of an intended double play, or forgetting a complicated rule, and so on. But this kind of stupidity in baseball does not include not knowing how you got on base. None of the stupidity in the source domain is used to project the stupidity in the target in this case.

It is not impossible to project stupidity from baseball to the target. One could say of Bush's having lost the election, although he was president during the dissolution of the Soviet empire, that he "got on third base without ever having hit even a single ball, and had the chance to steal home, but he blew it." But in "George Bush was born on third base and thinks he hit a triple," none of the stupidity in the target accords with a stupidity in the source.

Neither is the inference that Bush is a paragon of stupidity available from the target. It is nearly the human condition that we are all deluded about our position in life. If President Bush is deluded, he is not exceptional in this regard.

But, in the blended space of life as baseball, we have from the source the information that someone is on base, and from the target the information that he is deluded about his position or how he attained it. The blended result is being deluded about how one got on base. The counterpart in the source is impossible. The counterpart in life is the standard condition. But the projection to the blend is stupid in the space of life as baseball. The stupidity is in the blended space.[5]

The creative potential of the blend is highlighted by the following "joke," constructed on the basis of the comment about Bush on third base:

Dan Quayle was born on third base and thinks he kicked a field goal.

Here, the delusion extends even more unbelievably. The player thinks he is engaged in a different game. Given appropriate background knowledge about Quayle and football, we have no trouble constructing this novel blend, on-line. Understanding the joke requires creativity.

Conventional metaphors are commonly used to produce creative blends of this sort. Consider, for instance, the metaphor ANGER IS HEAT, analyzed by Lakoff and Kovesces. It gives rise to conventional expressions like *he's boiling mad, he's steaming with rage, he's about to explode.* But it can also be used more creatively, as in

He was so angry, I could see the smoke coming out of his ears.

5. Fauconnier and Turner 1994, sec. 4.

In the blended space constructed for this example, the boiling container is the head of the individual, the orifice is the ears, the smoke is the bodily manifestation of anger, and so on. The expression could not, of course, be literally true in either the source or the target of the conventional metaphor. In the target, angry people do not have smoke coming out of their body. In the source, smoke is liable to come out of containers like pressure cookers but not out of human heads. It is only in the blend that we have a coherent scene, which can map back to the source (as heat) and back to the target (as anger). Understanding the expression requires a creative blend, which exploits conventional mappings and background knowledge about smoke (in the source) and physiology (in the target: anger may be accompanied by physiological manifestations).

Creativity will operate on-line very generally. In our skiing example (section 5), the novice must produce a blended novel pattern of action on the basis of familiar inputs. That, in fact, is the instructor's motivation in prompting the construction of the blend. In cases of grammatical blends (section 6), speakers have the ability to integrate new causal sequences on the basis of the general blending schemas. For example, in the case of caused motion, we can understand expressions like:

They prayed the boys home.
The psychic will think Harry into another galaxy.
Jack choked the life out of his victim.
Junior sped the car around the Christmas tree.

All of these expressions correspond to different mapping possibilities for the blend. They give rise to very diverse emergent structure, and the surface syntactic structure does not directly reflect the semantic roles: It is the psychic who does the thinking but the car (not Junior) who does the speeding; and it is the victim, not "the life" that gets choked by Jack.

On-line creativity of conceptual integration is more noticeable when it operates at the narrative level over a stretch of discourse. This is in fact a frequent phenomenon. Oakley (1995) discusses at great length the following example of multiple blending and mental-space proliferation. It is taken from *Maus II, a Survivor's Tale,* by Art Spiegelman.

[Art is talking to his wife, Françoise, about his brother Richieu, whom he never met.]
   Art: I wonder if Richieu and I would get along if he was still alive.
   Françoise: Your brother?

Art: My Ghost-Brother, since he got killed before I was born. He was only five or six. I didn't think much of him when I was growing up. He was mainly a large, blurry photograph hanging in my parents' bedroom. The photo never threw tantrums or got in any kind of trouble. It was an ideal kid, and I was a pain in the ass. I couldn't compete. They didn't talk about Richieu, but that photo was a kind of reproach. He'd have become a doctor and married a wealthy Jewish girl ... the creep. But at least we could've made him go deal with Vladek. It's spooky having sibling rivalry with a snapshot.

This is a passage that we have no trouble understanding. Yet, as Oakley shows in detail, it builds up a complex lattice of blends, connected spaces, counterfactuals, and generics. On-line integration is the rule rather than the exception in the construction of meaning, but it is not usually as overtly noticeable as in Oakley's example.

Humor makes abundant use of blends. It is particularly obvious in the case of humor that listeners are intended to construct nonconventional on-line meanings. Coulson (1995) discusses such phenomena in some detail. One of her examples involves jokes about imaginary computer viruses named after celebrities and newsmakers. The brothers Menendez, tried for the murder of their parents, provided the input for one such joke:

MENENDEZ BROTHERS VIRUS: Eliminates your files, takes the disk space they previously occupied, and then claims that it was a victim of physical and sexual abuse on the part of the files it erased.

As Coulson shows, comprehension of the joke involves the construction of a complex blend, whose ultimate purpose is to project back to the source input, ridiculing the Menendez brothers' defense that they acted to protect themselves against abusive parents.

9. Principles of Integration

In addition to its overall structural characterization—cross-space mapping, selective projection in the blend, generic space, emergent structure, and so on—conceptual blending is subject to an array of competing optimality principles. Fauconnier and Turner (in preparation) show that there are different types of blend structures (*TF* structures, One-sided *TO,* Symmetric or Asymmetric Two-sided *TO,* Partially Unfilled *TO*). Such structures display different ways of optimizing the principles of integration. In addition, within one type of blend structure, some blends can be "better" than others because they satisfy more of the pressures, and many blends are ruled out in practice because of excessive violation. The following principles are proposed:

INTEGRATION: The blend must constitute a tightly integrated scene that can be manipulated as a unit.

WEB: Manipulating the blend as a unit must maintain the web of appropriate connections to the input spaces easily and without additional surveillance or computation.

UNPACKING: The blend alone must enable the understander to unpack the blend to reconstruct the inputs, the cross-space mapping, the generic space, and the network of connections among all these spaces.

TOPOLOGY: For any input space and any element in that space projected into the blend, it is optimal for the relations of the element in the blend to match the relations of its counterpart.

BACKWARD PROJECTION: As the blend is run and develops emergent structure, avoid backward projection to an input that will disrupt the integration of the input itself.

METONYMY PROJECTION: When an element is projected from an input to the blend and a second element from that input is projected because of its metonymic link to the first, shorten the metonymic distance between them in the blend.

These principles give rise to specific optimality pressures (nondis-integration, nondisplacement, noninterference, nonambiguity, . . .). The study cited above discusses many examples of the application of these optimality principles and pressures, and shows how they compete.

In summary, blending is a cognitive operation leading to creativity at many levels and in many areas of mental life. Yet it is a tightly structured and tightly constrained cognitive operation. In fact, it is presumably because it *is* structured and constrained in this way that human organisms are so deft at recognizing, manipulating, and producing it.

Conclusion

Perhaps the most surprising aspect of the organization of language and thought is the fundamental unity of the cognitive operations that serve to construct the simple meanings of everyday life, the commonsense reasoning of our daily existence, the more elaborate discussions and arguments in which we engage, and the superficially far more complex scientific theories and artistic and literary productions that entire cultures develop over the course of time. We have seen that the simplest meanings are in fact not simple at all. They rely on remarkable cognitive mapping capacities, immense arrays of intricately prestructured knowledge, and exceptional on-line creativity. They also rely on the impressive, and poorly understood, human ability to resolve massive underspecification at lightning speeds.

The cognitive operations focused on in this book have included cross-space mapping, access and spreading principles, space tracking by shifting viewpoint and focus, matching, structure projection, and conceptual blending. We are not conscious of performing these operations when we speak, think, and listen. Everything takes place very fast, and only the words themselves and the global emergence of meaning are accessible to consciousness. At other levels of thought, such as science, poetry, or rhetoric, there may be more awareness of some of the operations; we may consciously perceive an analogy, a metaphor, or a metonymy. Yet typically, even then, most of the efficient cognitive processes are hidden from view, and their overall structure is seldom directly apprehended.

Language is not a code for such operations. Their complexity far exceeds the overt information that a language form could carry. Instead, language serves to prompt the cognitive constructions by means of very partial, but contextually very efficient, clues and cues. Our subjective impression, as we speak and listen, is that when language occurs, meaning directly ensues, and therefore that meaning is straightforwardly contained in language. This fiction is harmless in many activities of everyday life—buying groceries or going fishing—but may well be quite pernicious in others—trials, politics, and deeper social and human relationships.

As in other areas of science, knowledge unveils ignorance. A glimpse of the elaborate mappings and blends that operate in meaning construction also reveals our vast ignorance of such processes. At this time, no one has a clear idea of how the brain carries out the high-level operations in question. And there is no computational model that captures the essence of analogy, blends, or domain matching.[1] Clearly, symbolic rule production systems are inadequate. The consensus is that a connectionist neural network architecture is closest to what the brain seems to be doing. And yet, in the areas studied in this book, there is multiple binding from one space to another, from roles to values, and from multiple inputs to blends. Multiple binding of this sort, structure projection, and gist extraction[2] represent formidable challenges to any modeling approach.

When we deal with a single language, the complexities of modeling meaning do not necessarily jump out, especially if the context has been artificially restricted to a microworld, as in Winograd's celebrated SHRDLU.[3] It is perhaps in the domain of machine translation that some researchers have become most acutely aware of what Oettinger (1963) aptly calls the "very mysterious semantic processes that enable most reasonable people to interpret most reasonable sentences unequivocally most of the time."[4] The reason translation reveals some of the hidden complexity is that different languages have developed different ways of prompting the required cognitive constructions. In addition, of course, different cultures organize their background knowledge differently. Good translation, then, requires a quasi-total reconstruction of the

1. Douglas Hofstadter, in his review of the book *Mental Leaps* (K. Holyoak and P. Thagard 1994), points to serious problems in contemporary modeling of analogy. Hofstadter's view is that the hardest part of analogical reasoning, gist extraction, is already done covertly by the analysts themselves in the way that they set up the inputs to their models. The modelers and those who evaluate their models are thus victims of a "giant ELIZA effect" (see Hofstadter 1995b).
2. As we saw in Chapters 4 and 6, only very partial structures get exploited for the purpose of analogy formation, metaphor, and blending. Extracting the right partial structures—the gist—from the considerable amount of structure and organization available for any real domain is beyond the capabilities of current models, which skirt the issue by focusing on the analogy process *after* suitable gist extraction.
3. Winograd 1972.
4. Cited in Dreyfus 1979. Dreyfus discusses very cogently some of the considerable problems posed by natural-language understanding for explicit computation or formalization. The phenomena we have studied in this book suggest that the obstacles to modeling are even greater than Dreyfus envisioned.

cognitive configurations prompted by one language and a determination of how another language would set up a similar configuration with a radically different prompting system and prestructured background.[5] It was long commonly assumed that this type of difficulty was a feature of literary translation, but that in everyday "objective" domains like commerce, science, or industry the differences would be tractable. This has turned out not to be the case, which comes as no surprise in the context of this book: The nature and complexity of the cognitive operations are the same in all cases.

When meaning construction is taken into account, the fundamental cognitive issues of learning and evolution appear in a different light. Clearly, what children learn is not language structure in the abstract. They acquire entire systems of mappings, blends, and framing, along with their concomitant language manifestations. If anything, the poverty of stimulus argument is even stronger for the learning of such elaborate systems than it is for syntax alone.[6] There is little doubt that children come into the world innately endowed with powerful capacities to develop such systems in the appropriate environments. But it is also true that the required cognitive operations function generally in thought and action. They are not specific to language, and the poverty of stimulus argument is not an argument for an autonomous language faculty. In fact, as we have seen repeatedly throughout the present work, the cognitive operations that play a central role in the construction of everyday meaning are the same operations that apply to reasoning, thinking, and understanding quite generally. There might, of course, still be purely structural language universals that hold independently of the system of meaning they help to deploy. But we cannot know this by studying word combinations in isolation, any more than we can understand the structural properties of addition or multiplication routines across cultures without reference to their mathematical function. For a child, to know a grammar is not primarily to know which strings are well-formed or ill-formed; it is to know how to apply partial grammatical instructions in context to produce appropriate cognitive configurations. For a cognitive scientist, linguist, or philosopher of language, to understand the nature of grammar, and to analyze specific grammars, is to provide explicit

5. Mandelblit 1995a.
6. Noam Chomsky has often argued that the evidence available to a child learning a language in a particular environment radically underdetermines the syntactic system actually learned by the child. See, for example, Chomsky 1972.

accounts of how grammatical constructions contribute in context to the elaboration of cognitive configurations.[7]

Most of the data in this book comes from language in the spoken modality. But there is now impressive evidence for the key role of mental spaces and mappings in signed languages (Liddell 1995a, 1995b; Van Hoek 1996; Poulin 1996).[8] Because the modality is different, overt linguistic manifestations of mental-space organization can be quite different and revealing in signed languages. Scott Liddell, in the works cited, has developed a powerful notion of grounded mental space. He shows how grounded conceptual spaces are part of our general thinking capacities, and how they are put to specific use, and grammatically signaled, in the anaphoric system of ASL. These important results fit in with our general theme that meaning at the most basic levels is supported and driven by general, not specifically linguistic, cognitive operations.

The other major cognitive issue is the question of how language appeared in the course of biological evolution. Here, we seem to lack the continuity often found for the development of organs and physical capacities. There is no record of species with rudimentary language abilities that would provide missing links between the absence of language and its full-blown instantiation in Homo sapiens. However, if we consider the bigger picture outlined in this book, there is perhaps more continuity than we thought. The essence of language, under the view I have presented, is the meaning construction system—mappings, frames, and spaces. The words and sentences are a surface manifestation of this complex activity. And there is every reason to think that the general cognitive processes we have considered are not restricted to humans. Other biological organisms (mammals in particular) engage in building frames, projecting structure, and making analogies, and many species have elaborate social structures and cultural models, aspects of which are internalized by individual members.

What human grammar reflects is a small number of general frames and space builders which can apply to organize the very large number of situations that we encounter or imagine. Through processes of integration

---

7. This very ancient tradition of language study—trying to explain what grammar does, not just what grammar looks like—has been revived in cognitive-functional linguistics (e.g., Langacker 1987, 1992, Deane 1992, Croft 1991, Fillmore and Kay, n.d., Fauconnier and Sweetser 1996). It goes far beyond the narrow characterization of syntactic well-formedness privileged by structuralist and generative approaches.
8. This line of research was first undertaken, in unpublished work, by Richard Lacy in the late 1970s.

and mapping, rich meanings can be constructed from symbolic assemblies that contain the required prompts for such constructions. Under this view, species differ as to their mapping capacities across domains and the level of abstraction they can reach. Language is a by-product of evolution along this dimension; it can emerge only when the degree of abstraction reached allows a small number of assemblies (coded by sound, sign, and gesture) to apply to multiple, objectively dissimilar situations.

This view is consonant with the surface discontinuity of language evolution. Until the appropriate capacity for abstraction, mapping, and conceptual connection is achieved, the conceptual system of an organism is, paradoxically, too rich and diverse for an efficient coding of general prompts for meaning construction.

References

Bloom, L. 1974. Talking, Understanding, and Thinking. In R. L. Schiefelbusch and L. L. Lloyd, eds., *Language Perspectives: Acquisition, Retardation, and Intervention.* Baltimore, Md.: University Park Press.

———. 1991. Representation and Expression. In N. Krasnegor, D. Rumbaugh, R. Schiefelbusch, and M. Studdert-Kennedy, eds., *Biological and Behavioral Foundations for Language Development.* Hillsdale, N.J.: Lawrence Erlbaum Associates.

Brée, D. S. 1982. Counterfactuals and Causality. *Journal of Semantics* 1.2.

Brown, A. 1990. Domain-Specific Principles Affect Learning and Transfer in Children. *Cognitive Science* 14:107–33.

Brugman, C. 1988. *The Story of* Over: *Polysemy, Semantics, and the Structure of the Lexicon.* New York: Garland Publishing.

———. 1996. Mental Spaces and Constructional Meaning. In G. Fauconnier and E. Sweetser, eds., *Spaces, Worlds, and Grammar.* Chicago: University of Chicago Press.

Carlson, G. 1979. Generics and Atemporal *When. Linguistics and Philosophy* 3:49–98.

Chomsky, N. 1965. *Aspects of the Theory of Syntax.* Cambridge, Mass.: MIT Press.

———. 1972. *Language and Mind.* New York: Harcourt Brace Jovanovich.

Churchland, P. 1986. *Neurophilosophy.* Cambridge, Mass.: MIT Press.

Cicourel, A. 1996. Ecological Validity and "White Room Effects": The Interaction of Cognitive and Cultural Models in the Pragmatic Analysis of Elicited Narratives from Children. Paper presented at the Fourth International Pragmatics Association Conference, Kobe, Japan.

Cornulier, B. de. 1985. *Effets de sens.* Paris: Le Seuil.

Coulson, S. 1995. Analogic and Metaphoric Mapping in Blended Spaces: Menendez Brothers Virus. *The Newsletter of the Center for Research in Language* 9.1.

Croft, W. 1991. *Syntactic Categories and Grammatical Relations.* Chicago: University of Chicago Press.

Cutrer, M. 1994. *Time and Tense in Narratives and Everyday Language.* Ph.D. diss., University of California, San Diego.

Dahl, O. 1976. Games and Models. In O. Dahl, ed., *Logic, Pragmatics and Grammar*. City: Publisher.

Dahl, O., and C. Hellman. 1995. What Happens When We Use an Anaphor? Stockholm University. Manuscript.

Damasio, Antonio R. 1994. *Descartes' Error: Emotion, Reason, and the Human Brain*. New York: G. P. Putnam.

Dancygier, B. 1992. Two Metatextual Operators: Negation and Conditionality in English and Polish. In *Proceedings of the Eighteenth Annual Meeting of the Berkeley Linguistics Society* 61:75. Berkeley Linguistics Society, University of California, Berkeley.

Dancygier, B., and E. Sweetser. 1996. Conditionals, Distancing, and Alternative Spaces. In A. Goldberg, ed., *Conceptual Structure, Discourse, and Language*. New York: Cambridge University Press.

Davidson, D. 1979. What Metaphors Mean. In S. Sacks, ed., *On Metaphor*, pp. 29–46. Chicago: University of Chicago Press.

Deane, P. 1992. *Grammar in Mind and Brain: Explorations in Cognitive Syntax*. Berlin and New York: Mouton de Gruyter.

Declerck, R. 1988. Restrictive *when*-Clauses. *Linguistics and Philosophy* 11:131–68.

Dinsmore, J. 1981. *The Inheritance of Presupposition*. Amsterdam: John Benjamins.

———. 1991. *Partitioned Representations*. Dordrecht: Kluwer.

Doiz-Bienzobas, A. 1995. *The Preterite and the Imperfect in Spanish: Past Situation vs. Past Viewpoint*. Ph.D. diss., University of California, San Diego.

Dreyfus, H. 1979. *What Computers Can't Do: The Limits of Artificial Intelligence*. New York: Harper and Row.

Edelman, G. 1992. *Bright Air, Brilliant Fire: On the Matter of the Mind*. New York: Basic Books.

Encrevé, P. 1988. C'est Reagan qui a coulé le billet vert. *Actes de la Recherche en Sciences Sociales 71/72*.

Espenson, J. 1991. The Structure of the System of Causation Metaphors. University of California, Berkeley. Manuscript.

Farkas, D., and Y. Sugioka. 1983. Restrictive *if/when* Clauses. *Linguistics and Philosophy* 6:225–58.

Fauconnier, G. 1975. Pragmatic Scales and Logical Structure. *Linguistic Inquiry* 6:353–75.

———. 1985. *Mental Spaces*. Cambridge, Mass.: MIT Press. Rev. ed. New York: Cambridge University Press, 1994.

———. 1986. Roles and Connecting Paths. In Charles Travis, ed., *Meaning and Interpretation*. Oxford: Oxford University Press.

———. 1990a. Domains and Connections. *Cognitive Linguistics* 1.1.

———. 1990b. Invisible Meaning. *Berkeley Linguistic Society* 16.

————. 1991. Subdivision Cognitive. *Communications* 53.

————. 1992. Sens potentiel: Grammaire et discours. In W. De Mulder, F. Schuerewegen, and L. Tasmowski, eds., *Enunciation et Parti Pris.* Amsterdam: Rodopi.

Fauconnier, G., and E. Sweetser. 1996. *Spaces, Worlds, and Grammar.* Chicago: University of Chicago Press.

Fauconnier, G., and M. Turner. 1994. Conceptual Projection and Middle Spaces. *UCSD Cognitive Science Technical Report.*

————. 1996. Blending as a Central Process of Grammar. In Adele Goldberg, ed., *Conceptual Structure, Discourse, and Language.* Stanford: Center for the Study of Language and Information (distributed by Cambridge University Press).

————. In preparation. Conceptual Integration.

Fillmore, C. 1982. Frame Semantics. In Linguistic Society of Korea, ed., *Linguistics in the Morning Calm.* Seoul: Hanshin.

————. 1985. Frames and the Semantics of Understanding. *Quaderni di semantica* 6.2:222–53.

————. 1990. Epistemic Stance and Grammatical Form in English Conditional Sentences. *Proceedings of the 26th Meeting of the Chicago Linguistic Society.*

Fillmore, C., and P. Kay. n.d. On Grammatical Constructions. University of California, Berkeley. Manuscript.

Fodor, J., and J. Katz. 1964. *The Structure of Language.* Englewood Cliffs, N.J.: Prentice–Hall.

Fujii, S. 1992. English and Japanese Devices for Building Mental Spaces. University of California, Berkeley. Manuscript. Paper presented at the International Pragmatics Conference, Kobe, Japan, in July 1993.

Gazdar, G. 1979. *Pragmatics, Implicature, Presupposition and Logical Form.* New York: Academic Press.

Geach, P. 1962. *Reference and Generality.* Ithaca, N.Y.: Cornell University Press.

Gentner, D. 1983. Structure-mapping: A Theoretical Framework for Analogy. *Cognitive Science* 7.2.

————. 1989. The Mechanisms of Analogical Learning. In S. Vosniadou and A. Ortony, eds., *Similarity and Analogical Reasoning.* New York: Cambridge University Press.

Gibbs, R. 1994. *The Poetics of Mind.* New York: Cambridge University Press.

Gick, M. L., and K. Holyoak. 1983. Schema Induction and Analogical Transfer. *Cognitive Psychology* 15:1–38.

Goffman, E. 1959. *The Presentation of Self in Everyday Life.* New York: Doubleday.

————. 1974. *Frame Analysis.* New York: Harper and Row.

Goldberg, A. 1992. The Inherent Semantics of Argument Structure: The Case of the English Ditransitive Construction. *Cognitive Linguistics* 3.1:37–74.

———. 1994. *Constructions*. Chicago: University of Chicago Press.

Goldstick, D. 1978. The Truth Conditions of Counterfactual Conditional Sentences. *Mind* 87.

Goodman, N. 1947. The Problem of Counterfactual Conditionals. *Journal of Philosophy* 44.

Grice, P. 1967. Logic and Conversation. Manuscript. (William James lectures at Harvard).

———. 1975. Logic and Conversation. In P. Cole and J. Morgan, eds., *Syntax and Semantics*. Vol. 3: *Speech Acts*. New York: Academic Press.

Harris, Z. 1951. *Methods in Structural Linguistics*. Chicago: University of Chicago Press.

———. 1952. Discourse Analysis. *Language* 28:1–30.

Hofstadter, D. 1985. Analogies and Roles in Human and Machine Thinking. *Metamagical Themas*, chap. 24. New York: Bantam Books.

———. 1995a. *Fluid Concepts and Creative Analogies*. New York: Basic Books.

———. 1995b. A Review of *Mental Leaps: Analogy in Creative Thought*. *AI Magazine* 16.3:75–80.

Hofstadter, D., G. Clossman, and M. Meredith. 1982. Shakespeare's Plays Weren't Written by Him, But by Someone Else of the Same Name: An Essay on Intensionality and Frame-based Knowledge Representation Systems. Bloomington: Indiana University Linguistics Club.

Hofstadter, D. et al., 1989. Synopsis of the Workshop on Humor and Cognition. *Humor* 2.4:417–40.

Hogan, L. 1995. Novel Blends in Contemporary English. University of New Mexico. Manuscript.

Holyoak, K., and P. Thagard. 1994. *Mental Leaps: Analogy in Creative Thought*. Cambridge, Mass.: MIT Press.

Humbert, P. 1957. Les mathématiques. In M. Daumas, *Histoire de la science*. Paris: Gallimard.

Hutchins, E. 1995. *Cognition in the Wild*. Cambridge, Mass.: MIT Press.

Indurkhya, B. 1992. *Metaphor and Cognition*. Dordrecht: Kluwer.

Jackendoff, R. 1975. On Belief Contexts. *Linguistic Inquiry* 6.1.

———. 1983. *Semantics and Cognition*. Cambridge, Mass.: MIT Press.

Karttunen, L. 1973. Presuppositions of Compound Sentences. *Linguistic Inquiry* 4.2.

Karttunen, L., and S. Peters. 1979. Conventional Implicature. In C.-K. Oh and D. Dineen, eds., *Syntax and Semantics*. Vol. 11: *Presupposition*. New York: Academic Press.

Kay, P. 1992. The Inheritance of Presupposition. *Linguistics and Philosophy* 15:333–81.

Kinsui, S., and Y. Takubo. 1990. Danwakanri Riron kara Mita Nihongo no Sijisi (Discourse management analysis of Japanese demonstrative expressions). In *Nintikagaku no Hatten* (Progress in cognitive science), 3:85–115. The Japanese Cognitive Science Society.

Kline, M. 1980. *Mathematics: The Loss of Certainty*. Oxford: Oxford University Press.

Koestler, A. 1964. *The Act of Creation*. New York: Macmillan.

Kuhn, Thomas S. 1962. *The Structure of Scientific Revolutions*. Chicago: University of Chicago Press.

Kunda, Z., D. T. Miller, and T. Clare. 1990. Combining Social Concepts: The Role of Causal Reasoning. *Cognitive Science* 14:551–77.

Lakoff, G. 1987. *Women, Fire and Dangerous Things*. Chicago: University of Chicago Press.

———. 1993. The Contemporary Theory of Metaphor. In Andrew Ortony, ed., *Metaphor and Thought*, pp. 202–51. New York: Cambridge University Press.

———. 1996. Multiple Selves. In G. Fauconnier and E. Sweetser, eds., *Spaces, Worlds, and Grammar*. Chicago: University of Chicago Press.

Lakoff, G., and M. Johnson. 1980. *Metaphors We Live By*. Chicago: University of Chicago Press.

Lakoff, G., and M. Turner. 1989. *More Than Cool Reason*. Chicago: University of Chicago Press.

Langacker, R. 1978. The Form and Meaning of The English Auxiliary. *Language* 54:853–82.

———. 1987. *Foundations of Cognitive Grammar*. Vol. 1. Stanford, Calif.: Stanford University Press.

———. 1988. An Overview of Cognitive Grammar. In Brygida Rudzka-Ostyn, ed., *Topics in Cognitive Linguistics*, pp. 1–48. Amsterdam and Philadelphia: John Benjamins Publishing Company. Published as volume 50 of the series Current Issues in Linguistics.

———. 1991. *Foundations of Cognitive Grammar*. Vol. 2. Stanford, Calif.: Stanford University Press.

———. 1993. Reference Point Constructions. *Cognitive Linguistics* 4.1:1–38.

Lansing, J. 1992. Mental Spaces and the English Progressive. University of California, San Diego. Manuscript.

Lewis, D. 1972. General Semantics. In D. Davidson and G. Harman, eds., *Semantics of Natural Languages*, pp. 169–218. Dordrecht: Reidel.

———. 1973. *Counterfactuals*. Cambridge, Mass.: Harvard University Press.

Liddell, Scott K. 1995a. Real, Surrogate and Token Space: Grammatical Consequences in ASL. In K. Emmorey and J. Reilly, eds., *Language, Gesture, and Space*, 19–41. Hillsdale, N.J.: Lawrence Erlbaum Associates.

———. 1995b. Spatial Representations in Discourse. Gallaudet College, Washington, D.C. Manuscript.

Lindner, S. 1982. What Goes Up Doesn't Necessarily Come Down: The Ins and Outs of Opposites. In *Papers from the Eighteenth Regional Meeting*, Chicago Linguistic Society, pp. 305–23. Chicago: Chicago Linguistic Society.

Maldonado, R. 1992. *Middle Voice: The Case of Spanish* se. Ph.D. diss., University of California, San Diego.

Mandelblit, N. 1995a. Beyond Lexical Semantics: Mapping and Blending of Conceptual and Linguistic Structures in Machine Translation. In *Proceedings of the 4th International Conference on the Cognitive Science of Natural Language Processing*. Dublin, Ireland, July 1995.

———. 1995b. Formal and Conceptual Blending in the Hebrew Verbal System: A Cognitive Basis for Verbal-Pattern Alternations in Modern Hebrew. Cognitive Science Department, University of California, San Diego.

Mandler, J. M. 1992. How to Build a Baby: Conceptual Primitives. *Psychological Review* 99.

———. Forthcoming. Representation. In *Cognition, Perception, and Language*, ed. D. Kuhn and R. Siegler. Vol. 2 of W. Damon, ed., *Handbook of Child Psychology*

Marconi, D. 1991. Semantica cognitiva. *Introduzione alla filosofia analitica del linguaggio*, pp. 431–82. Rome and Bari: Laterza.

Matsumoto, Yo. Forthcoming. Subjective Motion and English and Japanese Verbs. *Cognitive Linguistics* 7.2:183–226.

McCawley, J. 1981. *Everything That Linguists Have Always Wanted to Know about Logic*. Chicago: University of Chicago Press.

Mejías-Bikandi, E. 1993. *Syntax, Discourse, and Acts of Mind: A Study of the Indicative/Subjunctive in Spanish*. Ph.D. diss., University of California, San Diego.

———. 1996. Space Accessibility and Mood in Spanish. In G. Fauconnier and E. Sweetser, eds., *Spaces, Worlds, and Grammar*. Chicago: University of Chicago Press.

Mitchell, M. 1993. *Analogy-making as Perception*. Cambridge, Mass.: MIT Press.

Montague, R. 1973. The Proper Treatment of Quantification in Ordinary English. In K. Hintikka et al., eds., *Approaches to Natural Language*. Dordrecht: Reidel.

Morgan, J. 1973. Presupposition and the Representation of Meaning: Prolegomena. Ph.D. diss., University of Chicago.

Moser, D. 1988. If This Paper Were in Chinese, Would Chinese People Understand the Title? Center for Research on Concepts and Cognition, Indiana University, Bloomington. Manuscript.

Moser, D., and D. Hofstadter. n.d. Errors: A Royal Road to the Mind. Center for Research on Concepts and Cognition, Indiana University. Manuscript.

Norman, D. 1988. *The Psychology of Everyday Things*. New York: Basic Books.

Nunberg, G. 1978. The Pragmatics of Reference. Bloomington: Indiana University Linguistics Club.

Oakley, T. 1995. *Presence: The Conceptual Basis of Rhetorical Effect*. Ph.D. diss., University of Maryland.

Oettinger, A. 1963. The State of the Art of Automatic Language Translation: An Appraisal. In H: Marchl, ed., *Beitraege zur Sprachkunde und Informations Verarbeitung*. Munich: Oldenbourg Verlage.

Orlich, F., and J. Mandler. 1992. Analogical Transfer: The Roles of Schema Abstraction and Awareness. University of California, San Diego. Manuscript.

Poulin, C. 1996. Manipulation of Discourse Spaces in ASL. In Adele Goldberg, ed., *Conceptual Structure, Discourse, and Language*. Stanford, Calif.: Center for the Study of Language and Information (distributed by Cambridge University Press).

Putnam, H. 1975. The Meaning of 'Meaning.' In H. Putnam, *Mind, Language, and Reality: Philosophical Papers*. Cambridge: Cambridge University Press.

Reddy, M. 1979. The Conduit Metaphor. In A. Ortony, ed., *Metaphor and Thought*. Cambridge: Cambridge University Press.

Ross, J. R. 1970. On Declarative Sentences. In R. Jacobs and P. Rosenbaum, eds., *Readings in English Transformational Grammar*, pp. 222–72. Boston: Ginn.

Rubba, J. 1996. Alternate Grounds in the Interpretation of Deictic Expressions. In G. Fauconnier and E. Sweetser, eds., *Spaces, Worlds, and Grammar*. Chicago: University of Chicago Press.

Sadock, J. 1974. *Toward a Linguistic Theory of Speech Acts*. New York: Academic Press.

Sakahara, S. 1996. Roles and Identificational Copular Sentences. In G. Fauconnier and E. Sweetser, eds., *Spaces, Worlds, and Grammar*. Chicago: University of Chicago Press.

———. ed. 1990. *Advances in Japanese Cognitive Science*. Vol. 3. Tokyo: Kodansha Scientific.

Sanders, J., and G. Redeker. 1996. Perspective and the Representation of Speech and Thought in Narrative Discourse. In G. Fauconnier and E. Sweetser, eds., *Spaces, Worlds, and Grammar*. Chicago: University of Chicago Press.

Saussure, F. de. 1969. Cours de linguistique générale, publié par Charles Bally et Albert Sechehaye, avec la collaboration de Albert Riedlinger. Paris: Payot.

Schiebe, T. 1975. *Ueber Präsuppositionen zusammengesetzter Sätze im Deutschen*. Stockholm: Almquist and Wiksell.

Sereno, M. 1991a. Four Analogies between Biological and Cultural/Linguistic Evolution. *Journal of Theoretical Biology* 151:467–507.

————. 1991b. Language and the Primate Brain. *Proceedings, Thirteenth Annual Conference of the Cognitive Science Society*, pp. 79–84. Hillsdale, N.J.: Lawrence Erlbaum Associates.

Sweetser, E. 1990. *From Etymology to Pragmatics: The Mind-as-Body Metaphor in Semantic Structure and Semantic Change.* Cambridge: Cambridge University Press.

————. 1996. Mental Spaces and the Grammar of Conditional Constructions. In G. Fauconnier and E. Sweetser, eds., *Spaces, Worlds, and Grammar.* Chicago: University of Chicago Press.

————. Forthcoming. Reasoning, Mappings, and Meta-metaphorical Conditionals. In M. Shibatani and S. Thompson, eds., *Topics in Semantics.*

Takubo, Y. 1993. Danwakanri Riron kara Mita Nihongo no Hanjijitu Jokenbun (Discourse management analysis of Japanese counterfactuals). In T. Masuoka, ed., *Nihongo no Joken Hyogen* (Conditionals in Japanese), pp. 169–83. Tokyo: Kurosio Shuppan.

Takubo, Y., and S. Kinsui. 1992. Discourse Management in Terms of Mental Domains. Report for Monbusho grant No. 02300159.

Talmy, L. 1977. Rubber-sheet Cognition in Language. *Proceedings of the 13th Regional Meeting of the Chicago Linguistic Society.*

————. 1985. Force Dynamics in Language and Thought. *Papers from the Parasession on Causatives and Agentivity.* Chicago: Chicago Linguistic Society.

————. 1991. Path to Realization: A Typology of Event Conflation. State University of New York, Buffalo. Manuscript.

————. Forthcoming. Fictive Motion in Language and "ception." In Paul Bloom, Mary Peterson, Lynn Nadel, and Merrill Garrett, eds., *Language and Space.* Cambridge, Mass.: MIT Press.

Tarski, Alfred. 1956. *Logic, Semantics, Metamathematics; Papers from 1923 to 1938.* Oxford: Clarendon Press.

Travis, C. 1981. *The True and the False: The Domain of the Pragmatic.* Amsterdam: John Benjamins.

Traxler, M., A. Sanford, J. Aked, and L. Moxey. 1995. Processing Causal and Diagnostic Statements in Discourse. Human Communication Research Centre, University of Glasgow. Manuscript.

Turner, M. 1986. *Death Is the Mother of Beauty.* Chicago: Chicago University Press.

————. 1991. *Reading Minds.* Princeton, N.J.: Princeton University Press.

Turner, M., and G. Fauconnier. 1995. Conceptual Integration and Formal Expression. *Journal of Metaphor and Symbolic Activity* 10.3:183–204.

————. Forthcoming. Blending and Metaphor. In Y. Shen and A. Kasher, eds., *Cognitive Aspects of Metaphor.* Amsterdam: John Benjamins.

Van Hoek, K. 1991. *Paths through Conceptual Structure: Constraints on Pronominal Anaphora*. Ph.D. diss., University of California, San Diego.

———. 1996. Conceptual Locations for Reference in American Sign Language. In G. Fauconnier and E. Sweetser, eds., *Spaces, Worlds, and Grammar*. Chicago: University of Chicago Press.

Winograd, T. 1972. *Understanding Natural Language*. New York: Academic Press.

Index